FRESH AIR, BRIGHT WATER

Adventures in Wood, Field, and Stream

by Nelson Bryant

American Heritage Press New York

Book Design by Elaine M. Gongora

Copyright © 1971 by Nelson Bryant.
Published by American Heritage Press, a subsidiary of McGraw-Hill, Inc.
Published in Canada by McGraw-Hill Company of Canada, Ltd.
All rights reserved. Printed in the United States of America. No part
of this publication may be reproduced, stored in a retrieval system, or
transmitted, in any form or by any means, electronic, mechanical,
photocopying, recording, or otherwise, without the prior written
permission of the publisher.

Library of Congress Catalog Card Number: 74-145619
07-008605-2

To Vic,
who always outfishes me

Contents

Preface

Nearly four years ago when it was settled that I would write the Wood, Field, and Stream column for *The New York Times,* I was both delighted and apprehensive. How, I wondered, could one turn out approximately two hundred pieces a year that would interest substantial numbers of the *Times*'s far-flung and often sophisticated readers?

It was clear that I should not rely on the "where the fish are biting" approach that is expected of outdoor writers in local and regional newspapers, although some of that would be necessary, but rather that I should share the delights and glories of wood, field, and stream with my readers, giving the Westchester commuter, the Bronx housewife, the Connecticut doctor, the California lawyer an occasional glimpse of a mountaintop trout pond wreathed in mist, of black ducks flying low against a dark November sky over a brown salt marsh, of great, silvery tarpon rolling in the Caribbean, of red grouse rising above the purple bloom of Scotland's heather.

Part of the scene would be, I knew, the occasional killing of a bird or animal, and this gave me no anguish, for I have hunted and fished most of my life.

It may be that those who hunt for reasons other than survival are anachronistic, that civilization has made a once-honorable pursuit brutal, but I do not think so.

Most men and women who hunt and fish today are aware that the creature in the game bag or creel is only part of the ritual. Modern man desperately needs to get in touch with the tides, with the wind and the rain, with the forests and streams and mountains and their changeless and sustaining rhythms, and hunting or fishing is one way this is achieved.

There would be times, I knew, when columns would be devoted to telling of the growing horror of pollution, whether from sewage, pesticides, mercury, lead, factory smokestacks, or internal combustion engines, but it seemed that I might also serve our hope for a clean, new world by describing the simple pleasures and beauty, however tarnished, it still offers.

Nelson Bryant
Edgartown, Mass.

Spring

Middle Age Dulls Zest for Opening Day of Trouting

For more than thirty years, minus four lost springs during World War II, I never missed the opening of the trout season.

My devotion to opening day was a passion, a madness. As early as January I began work on my fishing gear, patching holes in boots, greasing lines, varnishing rod wrappings, repairing old flies and tying new ones.

In my boyhood, before I became addicted to fly-fishing, I was busy by the second week in March gathering night crawlers on warm evenings (the church lawn was particularly productive), digging common garden worms, and sometimes rooting in the manure pile by our barn for the little red worms that were the best bait of all.

Often my boyhood fishing companion and I couldn't wait for evening to go after night crawlers in the usual way with a flashlight. We fashioned a device from an old hand-cranked telephone, poured water around the worm holes to establish good conductivity, stuck two electrodes into the earth, and startled the worms out of their lairs with the resulting electrical shock. This had some success, as did pouring a mixture of dry mustard and water down the holes.

The brooks I visited as a boy were small, most of them, unsuited for fly-fishing; but the trout were fat and wild, and there were only five boys and one girl in my town who cared about fishing, a substantial proportion of our community's teen-age population at that time.

Opening day was usually below freezing at dawn. Ice formed in the rod guides, and in order to free the line I dipped the rod in the stream. Red-winged blackbirds clamored happily from the swamps, muskrat signs (and occasionally those of an otter) were all along the streams, and sometimes if the wind was right, or if there was no wind at all, I could hear the moaning of the surf on the South Shore three miles away.

As the years went on, the streams I fished were larger, my equipment became sophisticated, and my skill improved, but the magic of opening day began to wear thin.

Unless I had time to seek out some truly remote stream, I frequently had to share a one-rod pool, even if I got there first, with several other anglers, and the trout were no longer wild. Most of them had come from a hatchery truck a few hours before—pale, foolish creatures fed by man one day, caught by him the next.

Then, too, the early spring cold intensified the various aches and pains that one approaching middle age is heir to, and I found myself wondering, as I had never wondered before, why I wasn't home in bed.

A few years ago I stopped fishing opening day and the first few weeks of the season. After the first two or three weekends of trout fishing have gone by in the East, most of the anglers quit for the season. Good hatches of aquatic insects come along in May and June, making conditions ideal for the fly-fisherman, and the days are balmy and the natural world is blooming.

This is not to scoff at the pleasures men my own age, not yet half a century, derive from opening day. I watch them each year. Their fingers are blue, their legs ache from the cold water, they catch a few fish, and they are smiling. Cling, I say to them, cling to that boyhood magic if you can. I, alas, cannot.

4

Winter Quits New Hampshire Pond Grudgingly, But Spring Is Not Far Away

North Newport, New Hampshire

Winter leaves northern New England grudgingly. It leaves the cities, towns, and lowlands first. Snow melts on exposed hillsides and lawns; it is swept by wind and skiers from open slopes, and even though the forests are still deep in white, crocuses bloom against sun-warmed shingles and clapboards.

At Chapin Pond several days ago, only a few weeks from the vernal equinox, winter was in full command. A strong northwest wind hummed over the white, frozen expanse, driving ever-changing ghostly shapes of snow from one end of the pond to the other. The temperature was in the low 20's.

South of the pond, hardwoods—beech, oak, maple, birch, ash —bared their essential shapes to a brilliant blue sky, and among them there was no sound of life except for chickadees, whose merry voices are sometimes all a winter woods traveler hears.

During the four-mile snowshoe hike into the pond no animals were seen, although a few had left their signs. In one place the tracks of a grouse stitched across the snow-dusted crust, and a half mile down the trail there was a spot where another of his kind had spent the night buried in the snow, probably during a storm. He

5

had departed precipitately when a fox working up the wind smelled food. Wing marks on the snow marked where the bird had burst into flight, and two feathers showed that he had nearly been caught.

Later, when the trail was white pines, there were a few bordered by hemlocks and more tracks—cottontail and snowshoe rabbits, and a lone bobcat.

There were no deer tracks, nor could they be found by going off the trail on either side. The snow was thigh-deep, which was about normal for that time of year, and there was a crust that made it difficult for deer to traverse. The deer were probably yarded up in the big swamp northeast of the trail's entrance, where mixed hardwoods and softwoods provided forage within easy reach.

The pond was bare of animal signs, but under the ice at the western end, where the water was shallow and the ice had been thinned by relatively warm spring water trickling in, life was visible. Through that natural window, aquatic nymphs could be seen moving over the mud surface. Many would probably hatch as graceful mayflies in mid-June, but they also provided food as both nymph and adult for voracious trout now living in a half-sleep, occasionally searching for food but not needing much. Sometimes during a really hard winter, when the pond is tightly sealed by ice for long periods, many trout suffocate for lack of oxygen.

Living with the trout were salamanders, and in the organic muck of the pond bottom hundreds of frogs were deep in winter sleep.

In a month most of the ice will melt, songbirds will appear, spring freshets will tumble into the pond, skunk cabbages will thrust through patches of snow on the shore, sap will begin to move upward into the trees, and swelling buds will explode on pussy willows, dogwoods, alders, black birches. The creatures of the pond will move out of their near-death into pulsing, searching life, and on the shore and in the forests beyond, the warm-blooded animals will join the eternal ritual of spring, the cruel winter forgotten.

In Maine Bobcat Hunt, Hounds Ride behind Snowmobiles

Clayton Lake, Maine

By 4 A.M. only a small pocket of flickering coals remained in our wood-burning stove, and the bunk-house was cold.

A dust of snow had fallen during the night, enough, we hoped, to help us in tracking.

Included in our bobcat-hunting party of eight were four veteran "cat" men, Newton Stowell and Ralph Griffin, both of Dixfield, Missouri, Earl Hayward of New London, New Hampshire, and Gene Letourneau of Waterville, Maine. Others were Raymond Armandi of West Farmington, Maine, Norman Bernard of Livermore Falls, Maine, and Ben Pike, regional public relations representative for the International Paper Company. The IP's logging headquarters at Clayton Lake was our base of operations.

By midmorning we were aboard our snowmobiles and deep in the forest.

To the west, the area we covered extended twelve miles from Clayton Lake to the frozen St. John River and the once-thriving river community of Ninemile, now abandoned. Riding together to Ninemile, Armandi and I saw signs of deer, snowshoe rabbits, red squirrels, and fishers, but no bobcats. In some places it was possible for the smaller deer to move over the thick crust without breaking through, but the larger animals were forced to flounder in the snow, which was about four feet deep. This same crust made snowmobiling easy in the morning, but by midday, when the temperature went above freezing, the machines, particularly those carrying two men, were laboring.

At the river Armandi and I walked out on the flood-wracked steel bridge that can no longer carry vehicular traffic, and also visited the cabin of Camille Beaulieu, guide, trapper, and former resident of Ninemile. Beaulieu is also a mail carrier for the Clayton Lake area, which is in the northwest Allagash region.

During a midafternoon rendezvous east of the river, all members of the party came in with the same report: plenty of deer and fishers, but no bobcats. Later an old bobcat track was found, but the dogs were unable to make anything of it. (The hounds, which belonged to Stowell, Griffin, and Hayward, were Walkers, with the exception of one Redbone bitch.)

During the day each snowmobile covered forty or fifty miles. These machines have revolutionized bobcat hunting, once done only by men on snowshoes. The snowmobilers cruise logging roads and trails until a fresh cat track is found. The dogs, often towed behind the snowmobiles in boxes mounted on skis, are then loosed on the track. At this point the hunter straps on his snowshoes in order to follow his hounds through the thick timber.

Bobcats are bountied in Maine, as they are in neighboring New Hampshire. Their diet includes rabbits, squirrels, mice, birds, partridges, an occasional porcupine, and an occasional young or sick deer. Any bobcat over thirty pounds would be considered large.

I Will Never Know
If I Let That Big Trout
Escape on Purpose

One of the pleasures, and there are not many, of nearing middle age is, if one is fortunate, the growing store of pleasant recollections one can draw on.

Each spring as the time for trout fishing approaches I recall the big trout that got away in Mill Brook. It was more than thirty years ago that Albion "Beany" Alley, Jr., and I went forth together to fish for trout in Mill Brook on Martha's Vineyard Island.

We were, I must unabashedly report, using short metal rods, bait-casting reels, and worms. I had begun fly-casting a few years before, but had not yet reached the point where I could catch trout on a fly with any consistency, and the brook was really too small for fly-fishing.

We began fishing at Stepping Stone, a crossing about midway between the Mill Pond and the point where the brook enters Tisbury Great Pond, and took a few eight- and ten-inch trout each in the first fifty yards.

Once we frightened a pair of nesting native black ducks from a small flowage that came out of the nearby cranberry bog that belonged to Beany's grandfather, who was perhaps the best farmer the Vineyard ever had. We found an otter slide at the side of the brook and were pleased to note, by the size of the fish scales near the top of the slide, that the animal had been feeding on alewives, not trout.

The alewives, which had entered Tisbury Great Pond from the ocean two weeks before, were still in Mill Brook and were moving upstream to the barrier at Mill Dam, where they would spawn. Beany and I had already captured several hundred of the earlier arrivals in the pool below the dam, saving only the females for their roe, which is, to my mind, superior in taste and texture to that of the shad.

A few smelts were in the brook too, but the great smelt runs of a quarter of a century before had ended. A few years after the trip, the smelts disappeared altogether.

Beany was a good fisherman. He possessed an uncanny ability to find trout and often took fish from places I had passed by.

We fished the last pool before the brook widens out into Tisbury Pond and were lolling on a gravel bar in the shallows when Beany rose, stole quietly across the stream, and dropped his worm beneath the stump of a dead tree that hung out over the water. All around the stump the water was less than a foot deep, but there was a two-foot-deep hole under it and the bank to which it was rooted.

I had started to tell Beany he was wasting his time when he shouted and came stumbling backward toward me with a huge trout on his line.

Never one for ceremony, he yanked that great fish, which was three pounds, across the stream to the gravel bar. Then the old line he was using parted, and the trout was thrashing free in the shallows. I fell on it and I remember its muscular body twisting and writhing in my hands. Suddenly it was surging downstream into the pond, leaving a big wake behind.

I was a study in confusion—happy that such a splendid fish had not been dispatched so summarily and sad that my friend had lost the largest brook trout we had ever seen.

Beany looked at me accusingly as I rose dripping from the stream, started to ask a question, then decided against it. His silence saved me. To this day, I do not know whether I let that fish escape on purpose.

Minnow Seine a Handy Tool, But Sand Eels Are Elusive

What is the best net for capturing minnows for bait? A New England reader, looking toward summer, asked that question a few days ago.

Much depends on the area where one plans to use the net. If the spot is on the shelving, sandy beach of a bay, lake, or pond, a seine is undoubtedly the most effective. The usual minnow seine is four feet deep and varies in length; twelve or sixteen feet is usually sufficient unless one is planning a commercial endeavor.

The minnow seine, which has a fine quarter-inch mesh, is suspended in the water by floats on its upper edge and has a row of lead weights along the bottom. Two five- or six-foot sticks attached to each end of the seine complete the rig.

Two men are needed to operate a seine, although a child can be pressed into service on one end while the adult makes a sweep out into deeper water and then to shore.

The key to seining is to keep the bottom edge of the net ahead of the top edge so the leads won't trip, allowing the fish to escape.

For deep water or a rocky bottom, and the lone fisherman, the collapsible, umbrella type of net or the large dip net is effective. One may hold it still in the water until a school of minnows passes over it. Bits of clams, bread, or other bait may be placed in these nets to attract small fish.

For the lone fisherman, where the water is not too deep and the bottom not too rocky, the cast net is most effective. This is the net that appears in travel brochures frequently, always forming a perfect circle and always thrown by a brawny native of the South Seas.

To throw a cast net effectively takes a lot of practice. One should spend several hours practicing in the back yard before venturing forth on the water. It is almost impossible to describe the technique. The best way to learn is from someone already experienced in its use.

A few years ago while fishing off the Florida Keys I bought my first cast net, a small one five feet in diameter, and brought it back East full of hope. I planned to use it to catch silversides and sand eels, favorite prey of Atlantic mackerel, flounders, bluefish, and striped bass.

The larger silversides were easy to catch, but despite great persistence I was unable to trap any sand eels, and I could not understand why.

My youngest son answered this question for me by donning a mask and snorkel and watching the slender sand eels when the net settled over them. They all, he reported, squirmed through the net with ease even though its mesh was the finest I could find. For some reason, a seine with the same mesh captures sand eels, although many escape at the last moment.

Nylon seines and nets are fairly expensive but are worth, when obtainable, the extra cost. Cotton will rot after a few seasons; nylon nets are almost indestructible.

Whitebait, or Silversides, Prized in Europe, Neglected in U.S.

Thinking of whitebait yesterday afternoon and of how good a plate of them would be, I plunged into the newly published facsimile edition of Isabella Beeton's classic and monumental *Book of Household Management* (Farrar, Straus & Giroux, 1,112 pages, illustrated, $12.95) to see what she had to say about them.

The whitebait, or silversides, whose range along the East Coast is from Virginia to Nova Scotia, has been sadly neglected by Americans, but has long been prized by European gourmets.

Mrs. Beeton, who took four years to complete her book, begun when she was twenty-one and first published more than a century ago in England, knew the whitebait. Put them in iced water, she recommended, as soon as bought, unless they are to be cooked immediately. Dust them with flour, shake off the excess flour, and fry them in boiling lard, a few at a time, for about three minutes. Lay them on paper to absorb the fat and keep them warm. Stack them on a napkin and sprinkle with salt.

In a footnote to the recipe, Mrs. Beeton wrote in part: ". . . served with lemon and brown bread and butter, a tempting dish to the vast numbers of Londoners who flock to the various taverns of these places in order to gratify their appetites. . . . The ministers of the Crown have had a custom, for many years, of having a 'whitebait dinner' just before the close of the session. It is invariably the precursor of the prorogation of Parliament and the repast is provided by the proprietor of the 'Trafalgar,' Greenwich."

The whitebait (large specimens approach six inches in length) may be distinguished from the smelt by its dorsal fins, its longer anal fin, and its lack of an adipose fin. It has a more slender head than the mullet and larger eyes. It should not be confused with the sand eel, or sand lance. Their ranges overlap. Although about the same length as the whitebait, the sand eel has a slimmer body and a long, low, soft-rayed dorsal fin more than twice the length of the anal fin. Both species are prime forage fish for bluefish, striped bass, Atlantic mackerel, and summer flounders. I, for one, do not find the sand eel as tasty as the whitebait.

Neither the whitebait nor the sand eel needs any preparation other than washing before cooking.

The easiest way to catch whitebait is with a common minnow seine, one that is the standard four feet deep, about twelve feet long. Whitebait appear in shallow water along the East Coast in late spring or early summer and remain until late fall. (The terns, who also relish them, arrive a few weeks later and depart a few weeks earlier.)

Whitebait die quickly after capture, and it is best to keep them in a dry bucket covered with seaweed or a towel. If kept in water, particularly if it is warm, the delicate fish die and become soft in a few minutes.

There are various subspecies of silversides, and some taste better than others, but it is difficult to tell them apart.

Landlocked Striped Bass Swim through Forest of Drowned Trees

Summerton, South Carolina

In December schools of land-locked striped bass race across Lakes Marion and Moultrie here in the Santee-Cooper country, pushing silvery clouds of gizzard shad before them.

When fishermen spot gulls bunching up over the harassed shad, they start their outboard motors and head toward the action. On Moultrie this is a duplicate of a scene one might see any spring or fall on Long Island Sound, but on Marion there is a difference: the chase often takes place through a forest of drowned trees.

In 1941, when the waters of the Santee River began to back up behind the earth-filled dam, creating Lake Marion, engineers cut down trees along the edges of the lake-to-be, but as H. Morrison Davis, manager of the Goat Island Resort, puts it, "They were in a hurry for hydroelectric power and left the trees in the middle standing."

As he said this, the mist began to clear in front of his Lake Marion fishing and hunting resort, which has boats, guides, sites for camping trailers, and a two-thousand-foot airstrip, and before us we could see the ghostly shapes of the dead trees emerging.

"The lake is down about four feet now," Davis said. "When it's up, many of the trees are barely under water. I think the trees actually help. They have provided cover for fish. We have fine crappie fishing, for example, and right now we're picking them up around the sunken trunks of trees. The biggest crappie from the lake weighed five pounds. We've also got largemouth bass, white bass, bluegills, and bream."

However, Lakes Moultrie and Marion are best known for their landlocked stripers. Davis, who was born in the area, recalls that before the dam was built stripers were caught downstream on the Santee. When the impoundment began, some striped bass were apparently trapped above the dam, and in the year that followed they grew rapidly and reproduced.

The striper is an anadromous fish, a saltwater species that enters rivers and streams to spawn. Landlocked in the South Carolina lakes, the stripers follow their ancient ritual, leaving the lakes, their substitute for the ocean, each spring and running up the rivers that flow into Marion, the Congaree, and the Wateree to spawn.

The striper's ability to survive in certain fresh waters has been no secret for a long time. In the last century Seth Green, New York State's pioneer fish culturalist, wrote of this. The problem has been to find the proper combination of water depth and temperature.

Davis says South Carolina is assisting the landlocked stripers by allowing sea sunfish coming upriver in the spring to enter Lake Moultrie. Moultrie was created by a diversion canal from Marion, and its outflowing waters form the Cooper River, which enters the Atlantic at Charleston. The state also stocks stripers in the lakes. Moultrie covers sixty thousand acres, Marion one hundred thousand.

The largest striper caught in Marion weighed fifty-four pounds, Davis said, but the average is a little under ten. The limit is ten fish per day.

"We could go out right now and catch plenty of panfish, but if you want stripers, come back in December or May when we can show you some real good fishing," Davis said.

Now Is the Time
for Fly-Fishermen to
Get Their Gear in Shape

Now is the time for Eastern fishermen to prepare their gear for the coming spring.

The average fellow, unless he is unusually well disciplined, stuffed his tackle in a closet last fall and forgot about it.

Reels should be taken apart, cleaned, oiled, and greased. Rods should be checked to see if guides or windings need replacement or varnishing. Lure hooks should be sharpened. New leaders should be made or purchased, and lines should be inspected for sign of wear.

Fly-fishermen in particular have an elaborate chore before them. All the flies, whether dry, wet, streamer, or nymph, should be honed to needle sharpness. Many will need a touch of lacquer to hold frayed tying thread in place, and many will have bits of last year's leader material clinging to them. Matted hackles on dry flies should be steamed apart over a teakettle.

And if a fisherman has never learned to tie his own flies, now is the time to start. The best way to go about it is to seek the advice of a fellow fisherman who has mastered the art. If this is not possible, any good sporting goods store will sell a good fly-tying kit for ten to fifteen dollars. An authoritative, heavily illustrated textbook on the subject should be purchased also.

A beginner, unless he is unusually dexterous, should start with relatively large hooks and streamer patterns. If he begins with tiny dry flies, say sizes 20, 22 to 24, he will quickly conclude that the craft is too difficult to learn.

It is wise to tie half a dozen flies of one pattern before going on to another. In this manner, only the materials required for the job at hand need be kept on the workbench.

When a man gains enough skills to attempt the tying of small dries he should remember that good materials are all-important. Hackle, in particular, should be of fine quality and should be in various sizes. It does no good, for example, to put a hackle that was meant for a 12 hook on a 22. This is one of the first stumbling blocks faced by a beginner: his dry flies all come out the same size whether tied on large or small hooks. Material must be scaled down as the hooks grow smaller.

Some trimming of hackle is possible after a dry fly has been tied, but too much of this is not good. The tiny ends of the hackle fibers, which would be lost in the trimming, help keep the fly on top of the water.

The beginner should also stick to time-tested patterns. There is, as one's skill develops, an almost overpowering urge to create a new fly. But new patterns are best left to the experts, whether amateur or professional.

What patterns should a beginner tie? Ask any experienced trout fisherman this question and he'll offer, if pushed, a dozen he considers the best, but his list will differ from the one suggested by another man of equal experience. Read several books on the subject, talk to several good fishermen, and make up your own list. Never forget, however, that there are little-known flies that do very well in certain parts of the country. These regional patterns should not be ignored and often will produce fish when all else fails.

Beloved by Few, the Sucker
Is Always Good for the Garden

The white suckers' annual spawning run up Eastern streams is beginning, and some fishermen find them worthy of pursuit.

My first experience with this species of sucker, which can grow to thirty inches and eight pounds, was fifteen years ago on the Little Sugar River in North Charlestown, New Hampshire, about a mile upstream from its confluence with the Connecticut River. I was fly-fishing for rainbow trout, had taken one nice eleven-inch fish, and was preparing to try for another when the reddish-gold belly of a three-pound fish gleamed in an eddy behind a boulder. I worked the water around that boulder for ten minutes, believing that a trophy rainbow had somehow survived several seasons in the heavily fished stream. Then six more large fish darted past my boots, and I saw that they were suckers.

Forgetting the trout for a while, I tried to snag a sucker (they will, by the way, occasionally take a fly fished along the bottom), but failed. Eschewing sportsmanship completely, I flung a fifteen-pound rock at a fat sucker and was gratified to see it floating belly up down the stream. It was a female loaded with roe, which I extracted and carried home.

Fried roe of alewife or shad is excellent. Sucker roe is horrendous, and one might as well try to cook up a batch of firecrackers. A high proportion of the eggs explode.

Later that spring on the same stream I met an old country gentleman who was spearing suckers for his garden.

"Put a sucker under a tomato plant or a hill of corn and they'll grow so fast you have to duck back," this twentieth-century Squanto said.

The meat of the sucker is sweet, but even when filleted it is loaded with fine bones. One can run the fillets through a grinder, which chops up most of the bones, and this ground meat mixed with bread or cracker crumbs or mashed potatoes makes a good fish cake, which may then be fried.

Suckers and alewives are similarly constructed as far as the plethora of small bones is concerned, and a technique for cooking alewives espoused by a friend of mine, Albert West of Edgartown, Massachusetts, might also work with suckers.

Take the alewife as it comes from the water, without gutting or scaling, and place it on a heavily salted sheet of brown paper in a shallow baking pan. Spread another layer of salt over the fish and pour about a cup of vinegar over the fish. Sprinkle more salt on the fish, making sure that a good coating of vinegar-soaked salt covers it, and cook in a low oven for two or three hours. It is done when a thick, dark-brown crust has formed. This procedure, says Albert, softens the little bones, permitting them to be eaten. And if you've cooked a female, the roe will be a bonus.

Suckers may be readily captured by spearing, snaring, and netting, and they also provide good sport for the bow-and-arrow angler. Laws vary from state to state on the taking of these fish, and some areas have creel limits. There are not, to my knowledge, any legal restrictions against throwing rocks at suckers.

Oysters, Mussels, Clams
Brighten Any
Seaside Family Picnic

Seaside picnics needn't be a drab parade of sandwiches, soft drinks, and sunburn lotion.

Children and adults take readily to a combined picnic and shell-fish hunt and can be quickly trained to devour at least a portion of their harvest right on shore. All that is needed is enthusiasm, a few basic tools, and access to clam, mussel, or oyster beds.

Oysters can be opened at the beach and eaten raw, with or without lemon juice, ketchup, or some suitable sauce. If fires are permitted, mussels and clams can be steamed open in a pot and dipped in melted butter or garlic butter.

Where oysters are accessible to the wader, a bucket and a potato fork will do the job. Sneakers or boots should be worn to protect feet from sharp shells. If possible, pick single oysters. Those in clusters are also good, of course, but the clusters have to be separated later on.

During and after the spawning season, which usually occurs in early summer, oysters, while safe to eat, are thin and watery. Hence the taboo against gathering them during the months without R's. There are individual and local variations to this, however.

The common blue mussels are easily plucked by hand from the bottom or from rocks and pilings on which they congregate.

Steamer clams are more difficult to harvest because they lurk underground. Commercial clammers often use a jet of water to dislodge steamers from their snug beds. This is by far the most efficient technique for harvesting, but it is not legal in some areas.

The most widely used method for digging steamers is the simplest: digging by hand over the holes made by the long necks of the clams. Digging should be slow and easy, for if care is not taken fingers will be cut and fingernails broken by contact with old shells and other debris. Shovels or garden forks can also be used, although many clams are smashed in this manner.

Seacoast residents are always trying to find a better way to dig steamers. On Cuttyhunk Island, in Vineyard Sound, off Massachusetts, for example, a common toilet plunger is often employed to dislodge the clams.

Some of the heavy-shelled species of eastern seaboard clams, the giant surf clam, the mahogany clam, and the common quahog, lie either flush with the bottom or with a portion of their shells protruding. These clams may be gathered by anyone wearing a diving mask, snorkel, and flippers. The quahogs may also be located by treading over their beds in bare feet.

Quahogs (small quahogs are the justly famous littlenecks or cherrystones) may be eaten raw, and the same goes for the mahogany clams. The surf clams, while edible when raw, are simply too tough and too much of a mouthful for the average person. The adductor muscles of the surf clam are sweet and tender, however, and are good raw.

The amateur shellfisherman should invest in an oyster knife and a quahog knife. These little fixed-blade tools are inexpensive and save a lot of work and possible injury. An expert can open oysters and quahogs with an ordinary jackknife, but it is not recommended.

New Hampshire Salmon Sluggish, But There Are Compensations

Lochmere, New Hampshire

It was a day of small delights and no landlocked salmon. On the drive north to New Hampshire a black duck burst from a roadside swamp and flew beside the car, at forty-five miles an hour, for one hundred yards. He remained less than ten feet away, on the driver's side, then forged ahead, lifted, and banked right, away from the highway, turning his head and glancing back as if seeking approbation for his performance.

At the general store in the hamlet of Northwood, New Hampshire, the proprietor was seated on the edge of the counter repairing his metal-meshed smelt net. No, he said in answer to a question, he hadn't been salmon fishing—he didn't have free time during the day—but he could go smelting because that was done at night.

At the diner in Northwood, where a traveler can get two eggs, bacon, toast, and coffee for less than a dollar, one of the waitresses was sighing at spring.

"Yesterday it rained a little, but it was warm," she said, "and it's been beautiful weather for a week. It will go above seventy today."

"Yes, and it will be below zero by the end of the week," her less romantic coworker said.

But the one who embraced spring was not dismayed. Her customer served, she opened a road map on the counter and read aloud the names of faraway places. "In the spring," she said, "I always want to go somewhere. I don't care where. I just want to go." Then, when a logging contractor came in and asked for a cup of coffee, she smiled wistfully and put her map away.

At Lochmere the water rushed down from the dam at the foot of Winnesquam Lake and poured into Silver Lake, a few hundred yards away, in a frigid, brawling torrent.

A young man was fishing the fast water from shore with a spinning rod and worms. He had, he said, caught six salmon there since opening day.

He did not add to his total that afternoon, nor did this writer, who fished streamers and bucktails on a sinking fly line.

The water was so cold that even with woolen socks and insulated underwear under waders, a half-hour was the maximum immersion time. The routine for four hours was thirty minutes of casting followed by fifteen minutes of sitting on the bank in the sun until one's legs stopped aching.

At sunset, an hour's drive west of Lochmere, two shore fishermen and a man in a boat were trying for salmon at Georges Mills on Lake Sunapee. The ice had melted around the landing and some of the nearby docks, creating a good-sized patch of open water, and that seemed a good place to try the following day.

Fathers Must Learn Patience
When Sons Fish for Girls

$\mathbf{I}$f a father trains his sons in the gentle art of angling, then later watches despairingly as the lads learn that girls are sometimes more interesting than fish, he should adopt a philosophical attitude.

First, if he will only wait—perhaps five years, perhaps a decade —his boys will be back, having discovered that all that glisters is not gold.

If this same father has younger daughters, it is possible and proper to press them into service as fishing companions, with the understanding, of course, that they too will someday turn temporarily to other interests.

When introducing a child to angling, a very important step is to assure that there are plenty of fish about, and that the angling itself is simple. One should not, for example, attempt to instruct a child of eleven in the art of fly-fishing unless that same youngster has had a year or two of worming for pan fish.

In the beginning, it is all right to cast the line out and hook the fish before handing the rod to the child, but any tot of spirit soon perceives that this is something of a cheat and demands his own tackle. Given his own rod and reel, the child will remain happy and occupied for at least an hour learning to cast. Otherwise, if the fish are uncooperative, he will be bored beyond redemption.

In fresh water in the East, bluegills, crappies, yellow perch, and rock bass are among the easily caught species ideal for whetting a child's appetite. Along the coastal areas, the ubiquitous cunners can be found along all docks, pilings, and rocks. A notch up the sport-fishing scale from the cunner is the white perch.

This fish is actually a bass, our only bass with joined dorsal fins, nearly equal jaws, and faint side streaks. It ranges along the Atlantic coast from Nova Scotia to Georgia and is primarily found in brackish waters, although it has been introduced in fresh water, where it thrives, as a sport fish.

The rod and reel record for white perch is nearly five pounds, but the average fish is less than a pound. The white perch is a boon to winter-weary anglers because it begins its spawning runs up freshwater streams in March and April.

Fishing for white perch is usually an all-or-nothing affair. They travel in schools, and a fisherman usually catches many or none at all. Garden worms, clam worms, soft-shell clams, quahogs, surf clams, bloodworms, small minnows, and artificial lures, including flies, are effective on perch.

When a school of perch begins to bite, one should get the fish in and off the hook as soon as possible before the school moves on. When bait fishing, it is a good idea to throw in bits of worm or clam as chum to keep the perch about.

Fly-Fishermen Successfully Woo North Carolina's Wary Trout

Edgemont, North Carolina

White blossoms of the serviceberry signaled winter's defeat from the precipitous east slopes of the Blue Ridge Mountains. Harper Creek was clear as air, clear and cold, and the trout were hitting both dry flies and nymphs.

Dr. Reid Bahnson of Winston-Salem, North Carolina, who is a grower of orchids and a catcher of trout as well as a physician, warned that the fish would be as skittish as a schoolgirl on her first date, then promptly caught and released a small brown.

Bahnson, whose stream manners are impeccable, said graciously to his companion, "There's a large trout in there. Go ahead and try it."

Perhaps frightened by the capture of his smaller neighbor, the fish ignored all offerings, but that was no problem—there were dozens of similar pools ahead.

Harper Creek is a so-called native trout stream in the 45,000-acre Daniel Boone Wildlife Management Area of the Pisgah National Forest. There is a four-fish limit on Harper, and only an artificial lure with a single hook may be used. No fish under ten inches may be kept. (This four-fish limit applies to rainbows and browns, but in the upper reaches of the stream, where there are native brook trout, the usual seven-fish rule applies.) Angling in these management areas is allowed only three days a week, and a special permit, in addition to a regular license, is required.

Harper Creek and others like it in North Carolina's Great Smoky and Blue Ridge mountains are not the best trout streams in the United States, but many are very good, and they course through wild and lovely country. Harper makes its tumultuous way down the mountain through a boulder-strewn bed, past steep rocky cliffs, past stands of hardwood and an occasional conifer, past the lacquered green of rhododendron.

Deer tracks are on almost every sandbar along the creek, and there are foxes, bears, raccoons, and grouse in the surrounding forests. It is also possible to spend a day on streams such as Harper without encountering another fisherman.

At this time of year felt-soled waders are recommended. Later on, when the streams warm up, waders can be discarded, but felt-soled sneakers are needed for sure footing.

The dry fly Bahnson recommended was the female Adams. It took fish, as did various nymphs. Late in the day a Royal Coachman was effective. We fished the stream by sections, with Bahnson going on ahead and leaving a few rhododendron leaves on a midstream boulder to mark where he had begun.

In the three-mile climb from the falls to Yellowbuck Trail, we caught perhaps forty trout, releasing all but two browns of 15½ inches, and thirteen caught by the doctor.

Those browns proved fine eating, having none of the muddy taste they often pick up in warmer streams. Most of the released fish were small rainbows, from five to nine inches, although there was an occasional little brown. The two species were planted in the stream a few years ago and had maintained their numbers through natural reproduction.

Unable to Sleep, Fisherman Walks Outer Banks in the Moonlight

Nags Head, North Carolina

A gentle wind came through the open windows of our room at the Carolinian Motor Hotel, forming beads of moisture on the screens and carrying with it the sound and smell of the sea.

Unable to sleep, I rose, dressed in the dark to avoid disturbing my fishing companion, Joel Arrington of Raleigh, North Carolina, and walked one hundred yards to the beach. It was after 2 A.M., and a nearly full moon shone down on the heaving Atlantic and on the lonely, lovely miles of barrier dunes, North Carolina's Outer Banks, that stretch 150 miles from the Virginia border to Cape Lookout.

I was grateful for the moon's illumination; it washed land and water with a holy light and enabled me to give a wide berth to occasional couples who lay close embraced in the warm night.

Arrington, outdoor editor of the Travel and Promotion Division of the state's Department of Conservation and Development, and I were attending the annual spring meeting of a loosely knit but happy organization known as the Honorary Tar Heels.

The previous afternoon, with Don Carpenter of Annapolis, Maryland, we had fished nearby Oregon Inlet from shore for bluefish, summer flounders, and hopefully, striped bass.

The blues were in the inlet but too far offshore for us to reach by casting, and there wasn't time to drive back to Nags Head and launch Arrington's boat. Flounders, however, were present in great numbers a few feet from shore, and we had no difficulty catching them. They fell victim to a variety of metal lures, including shad darts worked along the bottom.

One small striper, or rockfish as they are called along the coast from Maryland south, was beached, having found a slate-colored Alou bait tail to his liking.

The bluefish in the inlet were small, running one to two pounds, but giant blues have already been taken offshore in this area this season as well as blue and white marlins.

From June 7 through 13, anglers will converge on the Outer Banks for the eleventh annual international invitation blue marlin tournament, which is based at the Hatteras Marlin Club, Hatteras. During last year's tournament twenty-four blue marlins were boated and two released. The average weight was 388 pounds. Nine white marlins were caught and all but one released.

One need not own or charter a large boat to find good fishing along the Outer Banks, however. Channel bass and bluefish are often in the surf, and striped bass, sea trout, spots, croker, tautogs, and flounders are in the vast shallow, brackish sounds behind the dunes.

There are many well-equipped marinas where one may launch his own boat or rent or charter small craft. One may also pay a small fee and fish from piers that jut out into the Atlantic. Party or "head" boats are also available. Accommodations range from the camping areas on the Cape Hatteras National Seashore to thoroughly modern and comfortable hotels and motels such as the Carolinian.

Information on fishing, camping, golfing, restaurants, and accommodations in the Dare County area of the Outer Banks, which begins north of Nags Head and runs south to Hatteras Inlet, may be had by writing Aycock Brown, Manteo, North Carolina 27954.

While Sirens Scream, Anglers Catch Trout in Boston Pond

Boston

An ambulance howled down the highway on the west side of Jamaica Pond as we fished, weaving in and out of the traffic; lovers sat in the sun on the grassy shore, holding hands; and an elderly man tossed bread to several mallard ducks as a youth in a sweatsuit jogged by.

Jamaica Pond covers sixty-three acres in Jamaica Plain, Boston. Its clear, deep, and cold waters hold rainbow, brown, and brook trout, and bass, both largemouth and smallmouth. Here there is no whispering of wind in the pines or backdrop of towering mountains. Here is the throb and hum of a metropolis and a high-rise apartment looming in the north.

The pond is one of several city-surrounded trout waters in the Northeast District of the Massachusetts Division of Fisheries and Game. Some of the others are Plug Pond and Round Pond in Haverhill, Forest Lake in Methuen, Dug Pond in Natick, and Horn Pond in Woburn.

"In my four counties, Essex, Middlesex, Norfolk, and Suffolk (Boston), I've got three and one half million of the state's total population of five and one half million," said Richard Cronin of Harvard, Massachusetts, wildlife manager of the Northeast District. His area runs from the New Hampshire–Massachusetts border to the Bay State's North Shore, from near-wilderness to teeming cities.

On the way from Cronin's home to Jamaica Pond, we stopped at Walden Pond in Concord, an excellent trout water. Small signs pointed the way to the site of Thoreau's hut, but we did not follow them. We lay on our bellies on the concrete pier and watched rainbow trout swimming about in the clear water. There were perhaps twenty fishermen on the shores of the fifty-three-acre pond.

Walden, which yields a good number of large, holdover trout each season, is subject to intense fishing pressure during the first few days of the season, but later on there is usually plenty of room.

Leaving Walden, we drove to Jamaica Pond, past the forests of urban America, to the Jamaica Pond Boathouse.

There we found the boathouse's proprietor, Allen Curtis, seated with some cronies around a large, smoke-blackened fireplace. The boathouse has been in the Curtis family since 1912. Curtis rents rowboats to fishermen for fifty cents an hour. The rate is seventy-five cents an hour for recreation rowing.

The pond is within the Boston parks system, and one must have a permit, which is free, from the parks commission, as well as a regular license, to fish it.

Allen Curtis, Jr., rowed me about the pond as I cast flies for trout. There were no fish rising, but I did manage to catch three small bass and seven encouraging comments from youths lounging on benches.

"I'm afraid it's a worm or salmon egg situation," said young Curtis, "or if you could stay until evening there would be some action."

A nearby boat supported his thesis. In it were two young men who had a fine string of fine trout, mostly rainbows that they had dredged up from the bottom with worms. But no self-respecting fly-fisherman uses worms. If he did, he would have no excuse for failing.

When a Lobster Outgrows Its Shell, the Shell Is Left Behind

Oak Bluffs, Massachusetts

A woman squirming out of a tight dress could learn something from *Homarus Americanus,* the common lobster.

Many times during the course of its life, which might cover half a century, and without the aid of a zipper, the lobster (male and female) crawls out of its shell during the molting period, escaping through the joint between the tail and the carapace, then immediately begins to form a new shell, one that will accommodate its rapidly expanding body.

This and other bits of lobster lore were related by John Hughes, director of the state lobster hatchery and research facility on Lagoon Pond.

Since 1951 Hughes and his coworkers have hatched, reared, and released millions of lobsters into the coastal waters of Massachusetts and other New England states.

Rearing lobsters is difficult. They require constant attention, and mortality is high. About 22.4 per cent of the lobster fry at the Oak Bluffs hatchery survive through the fourth molt. At that point they are from nine to thirty-three days old. Cold water retards development.

Lobsters reach sexual maturity in five or six years, when they weigh about a pound. The age of a lobster is always an approximation. They have no scales or otoliths, as do fish, to provide a calendar of their years.

Mating must occur within a few days after the female has shed her tough exterior. Nine months later the female extrudes fertilized eggs, and they remain attached to the underside of her tail for another nine months until they hatch. During the egg-under-tail period, she keeps close watch over her brood-to-be, which may number up to forty thousand, removing dead eggs that could contaminate the others.

Hughes obtains egg-bearing females from commercial fishermen who have been issued special permits. (There is a one-hundred-dollar fine for keeping an egg-bearing lobster in Massachusetts. The clusters of greenish-brown eggs are clearly visible.)

Hughes has discovered that lobsters can grow new claws, but there is evidence that the replacement of a claw by a lobster retards it's overall growth.

Hughes bridles when anyone suggests that a lobster is, as Herman Melville wrote of the pilot fish, a "ravener of horrible meat."

"Lobsters are no more scavengers than we are," says Hughes. "Lobster men know that pots baited with rotten fish won't produce. The adult lobster's diet includes small fish, mussels, and clams."

Hughes feeds his lobsters bits of quahog meat, viscera of scallops, and fish, all fresh.

Because lobsters shed their shells often, no good method of tagging them has been developed. Thus Hughes has no way of knowing how successful his plantings have been.

He is trying to raise a special breed of red lobster. If he is successful, these could be released into a limited area, and subsequent catches would tell the story.

Lobsters are basically nonmigratory, Hughes says: 99 per cent of them remain within a one-mile radius of the spot where they became adults, provided, of course, that they are on suitable habitat.

Some Pesticides Threaten Man Himself, As Well As Fish and Fowl

The visible degradation of our natural environment—smog, slums, poorly planned highways and buildings, and once-clean rivers fouled with industrial and domestic waste—is all too apparent.

But this, while distressing, may fade into relative insignificance when placed beside the hidden yet pervasive corruption of the world's ecological system by so-called hard pesticides—DDT and Dieldrin, to name two. DDT has a half life of ten years, that is to say, half of any quantity of this broadly toxic pollutant breaks down in a decade, and the remainder halves again each year for perhaps a century. It is everywhere in our environment. Nothing we eat or drink is free from it. It is in oceanic fish, it is in birds and animals, it is in the milk a nursing mother gives her child.

Last Saturday at Hunter College, guests and members of the American Littoral Society learned that DDT was apparently to blame for the death of hundreds of thousands of young coho salmon from Lake Michigan and was also apparently threatening, through inhibition of reproduction, the extinction of a tiny band of petrels that live on rocky islets of the Bermuda group.

The death of the salmon or the extinction of the petrels is not in itself of vital significance to the world, although the end of any species is a minor tragedy, and the crippling of the Michigan salmon project, which was perhaps the most brilliant success of its kind in history, is not good.

Of fundamental importance is that man in his attempt to control his environment—in this case an effort to eradicate certain undesirable insects—has debased the food chains that sustain fish, fowl, animals, and ultimately man himself.

For example, one thinks of oceans as vast and clean, throbbing with life, and this is true. But already an insidious invasion of the oceanic food system has begun. DDT is carried to the oceans by rivers; it falls with the rain. It is found in the Antarctic, the Pacific, the Atlantic. It is not soluble in water and it moves into phytoplankton, the base of the marine food pyramid. As it goes up that pyramid to higher forms of life, it tends to become more concentrated.

To put it another way, the plankton contains some DDT, the plankton-feeding fish more, and more yet is found in the carnivorous fish and birds. Man, the highest carnivore, is at the top of all this.

Tests have shown that DDT in sufficient quantities has a disastrous effect on phytoplankton, stopping its photosynthetic processes. This may also create a side effect: it may leave a gap for other forms of plankton to "bloom," or hurtle into prominence. The ultimate effect of such a profound change, if it should come to pass, is not known. (It should be made clear, however, that the concentrations of DDT required to do this are far beyond those presently found in our natural environment.)

What DDT does to man is not clear, although there is evidence that it can cause irregular growth and cell destruction. There is little doubt that it inhibits successful reproduction in some birds and causes fatalities in the young of some fish.

It seems abundantly clear that until adequate research has established the full biological effects of DDT and other "hard" pesticides, their use should be stopped. It is possible, although not probable, that we have already gone too far. Some of the pesticides used today will be exerting their influence on our environment a century from now.

(This column was published in March, 1968.)

Eels Will Soon Start Their Long Journey from the Sargasso Sea

Every spring countless young eels end an incredible one-year journey from their birthplace in the Sargasso Sea, southeast of Bermuda, to the rivers and streams of the Atlantic and Gulf coasts of the United States.

At the same time the little American eels began their long, drifting swim, their close relatives, the European eels, left the same area and started a three-year trip to Europe.

Once in fresh water, the female American eels set up housekeeping, preferably on a mud bottom, and remain there from five to twenty-five years until they are sexually mature. At that time the males and females return to their birthplace, spawn, and die. There is evidence that the male does not usually swim as far upstream as the female. He frequently waits in an estuarine area and joins the female when she begins her journey back to the Sargasso Sea.

In Europe the common eel is highly prized as food, but most American housewives, perhaps repelled by its snakelike form, have never been fond of the eel, and consumption of this unusual fish in the United States is for the most part limited to specific ethnic groups at specific times of year.

Single eels may be readily caught on hook and line, and large numbers are captured with baited pots or with weirs. An eel weir is a fence (or fences), set along the shore of a river or pond, that guides the migrating sexually mature creatures, known as silver eels at that stage, into a large, torpedo-shaped pot with a funneled opening.

Migrations occur in the fall, and if the pond the eels are leaving has become landlocked, they will migrate overland at night.

In winter eels burrow deep in mud, and on the New England coast a time-honored method of capturing them at such a time is with an eel spear. A hole is cut in the ice, and the spear, a multitined affair with a long handle, is jabbed into the mud.

The semicomatose eels are caught in the tines and pulled to the surface. It takes a little practice to be able to tell when an eel is struck, and frequently six or eight of them will be found in a spot a foot square.

If kept cool, eels will remain alive for a week or more in a bucket without water. This survival capacity made them an ideal source of fresh food in days of no refrigeration.

Daniel Manter, a long-time builder on the island of Martha's Vineyard, once told me of a man who stopped by the farmhouse of a woman who lived on one of the island's saltwater ponds many years ago. After accepting her invitation to lunch, he watched her snatch a few squirming eels from a bucket beside the stove and slap them into a frying pan. This was somewhat crude. Eels should be skinned before frying.

The best procedure for a neophyte is to nail the eel's head to a fence, make a circular cut through the skin just behind the gills, and peel the skin off as one removes a glove. Before skinning, the slime can be stripped from the eel with a handful of sand.

And if you want to try something other than frying, the first American edition of *Larousse Gastronomique* has nearly fifty recipes devoted to this neglected food fish.

A Lovely Girl on a Lonely Stream Is Only an Angler's Dream

A picture of a pretty girl in a bikini standing beside a glassy-eyed, 54-pound 8-ounce king mackerel was recently mailed to me by Lefty Kreh, manager of the annual Metropolitan Miami fishing tournament.

The girl, Mari Lawlor of 420 East Sixty-fourth Street, New York, says Lefty, will receive a citation for her catch.

After studying the fish for several minutes, I noticed Miss Lawlor and was reminded of my youth. In my salad days, when hope and judgment were equally green, I often thought of finding such a girl on a trout stream.

Those were the days, Lefty, the days when I said to myself, "Just around the bend in the stream where that big hemlock stretches out over Twin Rock Pool, she will be standing, clad in waders and a little suede jacket, with a pert hat on her lovely head. She will be watching a big brown trout rising behind the most distant rock, 'Hello,' she will say in a voice as melodious as water over smooth pebbles. 'See that big fellow over there? I'm resting him now. I've been trying to raise him for an hour.' "

In my daydream I picked a bit of fur and feathers from my fly box and said, "Try this. I tied it myself for this stream at this time of year."

Her clear, honest eyes measured me candidly. "Thank you," she said. "You're very kind. I like men who tie their own."

As she fastened the fly to her leader, I asked, "Do you fish this stream often?"

"This is my first time on it. I live in Wappingers Falls. But I'm coming back. It's a lovely stream. By the way, my name is Alison Anapest."

It seemed impossible that this lovely girl was the Alison Anapest from Wappingers Falls whose best-selling narrative poem, "Lover with Hard Hands," had left reviewers gagging on laudatory adjectives a month before.

She saw the question in my eyes.

"Let me love, let me kiss, let me dream," she began, and, overcome, I broke in, finishing the opening lines of her poem for her:

"Let my lover be strong,
  let him ride
Through the storm, through
  the wind, in the sun,
His hard, brown hands
  gentle only for me."

We stood close. The big trout rose and hauled under a just-hatched mayfly. A hawk screamed high overhead, and the world was breathless and ours alone.

Well, Lefty, the nearest I ever came to such a confrontation was six years ago on Long Pond in Croydon, New Hampshire. I was struggling to load a huge old water-soaked 250-pound canoe on top of my car when a panel truck pulled up and a girl who weighed about what I do, two hundred pounds, climbed out. Her clear eyes —she was over six feet tall—looked down into mine.

"Let me give you a hand, Bud," she said and hoisted one end of the canoe over her head.

"Want help with yours?" I asked weakly after the canoe was on my car, but she seized her car-top boat, walked with it to the water, and set it down without a ripple.

"You ought to get a boat like this. You're gonna bust a gut one of these days," she said, hitching up her belt.

Ray Bergman's Collected Works Stir Memories of His Classic Trout Book

The late Ray Bergman meant a great deal to me, even though I never met him. Bergman, who died in 1967, was angling editor of *Outdoor Life* for more than a quarter-century, and his authoritative advice in that publication was read by millions.

I was a fan of Bergman's *Outdoor Life* writings, but his classic book, *Trout,* first published in 1939, was what first captivated me.

I did not learn of *Trout* until after World War II. Before the war I had attempted to learn all I could about trout fishing, particularly fly-fishing, but there were few anglers in my seacoast home town who knew much about the art, and it was surrounded with an almost impenetrable mystery. Then after the war, someone told me of Bergman's book, and I was launched.

The charm of *Trout* and all of Bergman's writing is authority, lucidity, integrity, and humility. He never pontificated, he never boasted, and he always reduced potentially complicated fishing problems to common-sense terms. He was no wild-eyed purist. He was, for example, not averse to using lures or bait for trout if flies did not produce.

For these reasons and many others, the publication by Alfred A.

Knopf of *Fishing with Ray Bergman* ($8.95, 328 pages, illustrated) is welcomed. Edited by Edward C. Janes, Eastern field editor of *Outdoor Life,* the book is a collection of Bergman *Outdoor Life* articles on the taking of the better-known species of freshwater fish, and it gives young fishermen the opportunity to meet the old master, and older anglers the chance to renew a valued acquaintance.

It was Bergman who drove home to me the importance of "reading" a stream, of knowing where the trout lie and of determining the best location from which to reach them.

One of the chapters in *Trout* describes how Bergman spent part of a day watching newly arrived fly-fishermen approach a certain trout pool. In analyzing their mistakes and achievements, Bergman taught me that ten or fifteen minutes or half an hour spent in observing a good stretch of water might mean the difference between success and failure.

In his foreword to *Fishing with Ray Bergman* Bill Rae, the editor of *Outdoor Life,* mentions that when Bergman retired from the magazine in 1959 he said that he wanted to rest, free of the column-a-month deadline he had been observing for twenty-six years, then do one more book.

The book, alas, was never written, and to his wife, Grace, he said one day, "I can't do it, Grace. I wanted to so much, but I can't do it."

This new book, carefully edited by Janes, is the nearest thing fishermen will ever have to the last book Bergman wanted to write. I, for one, am grateful for it.

Oil Spills Can Be Traced to Source through "Fingerprinting" Technique

Woods Hole, Massachusetts

In the last few years chemists have discovered that all crude oils and the products refined from them reveal, when subjected to gas chromatography, a distinctive "fingerprint."

Using this technique, scientists could identify the sources of ocean oil spills so that the offenders could be apprehended.

When President Nixon signed the Water Quality Improvement Act of 1970, the work of these chemists, including Dr. Max Bluner and his associates at the Woods Hole Oceanographic Institution, took on new significance.

The new law sharply increases the penalties for oil spills from offshore and onshore oil installations and from tankers.

Under a 1966 revision of a 1924 law, the government had to prove gross and willful negligence when prosecuting oil-spill cases. This revision so handicapped government lawyers, according to a spokesman for the Federal Water Pollution Control Administration, that they gave up their efforts to obtain convictions under that law.

The new law establishes absolute liability for cleanup costs except for an act of God, an act of war, negligence by the United States, or action by a third party, and provides fines for discharging oil knowingly into the water or failing to report a spill.

Says Bluner: "Each oil from each oil field, and very often each oil from each producing horizon (level) within the field is, in a sense, an individual, and when the oils go through processing and refineries, the products also have different histories. The histories influence the composition so that again, through manufacturing, the oils have a different composition. The 'fingerprint' of that composition can be recognized by analysis with sophisticated, modern analytical techniques like gas chromatography.

"In essence, gas chromatography brings about separation of the different components of the crude oil, according to their volatility."

Bluner said he believed that this and similar approaches to identifying oil spills on beaches and the high seas were first proposed in 1968 in papers published by Shell Research, Ltd., and the research center of the British Petroleum Company, both in England.

Ideally, those given the task of linking a spill with its source should have a catalogue of fingerprints of all the crude oils of the world and all the refined products of those oils, so comparisons of the known and the unknown could be made.

In practice, Bluner feels a much smaller catalogue would probably suffice, containing, for example, the major oils transported in major shipping lanes.

"There are certain things you can say without a catalogue," Bluner says. "You can say this is a fuel oil, this is whole range crude oil, or this is a product, this is a blend, this is a sludge." (A sludge is the oil-wax residue left in a tanker after its cargo of crude oil has been discharged; because it is difficult to dispose of in port, it is sometimes pumped out at sea.)

"I think," says Bluner, "that the only thing that needs to be done is to standardize the methods so they are carried out comparably in different laboratories. Adapt the methods to a field procedure that is sufficiently rapid to produce an analysis, for instance, within an hour after the oil is received, and then the build-up of a catalogue and knowledge."

This oil-sleuthing would not, Bluner observes, be merely punitive in effect. In some cases, analysis would remove a pall of suspicion from an innocent party.

Environmental Defense Fund
Fights Polluters in Court

The Environmental Defense Fund, Inc., a nonprofit organization of conservationists, scientists, and lawyers dedicated to the protection of our environment, needs assistance in its efforts to obtain working funds through public membership.

One of the E.D.F.'s better-known continuing projects is its efforts to stop the use of DDT and other persistent pesticides in the United States. Largely through E.D.F. efforts, DDT has been banned in Michigan, Wisconsin, and several other states.

On the national level E.D.F., joined by other conservation organizations, has litigation against two federal agencies under way in a federal court in Washington to gain further restrictions on the use of DDT. In a recent newsletter E.D.F. said that it would continue the fight until DDT and its cousins were not only controlled but totally banned.

E.D.F.'s concern is not limited to pesticides: the organization has filed suit against a major air polluter in Montana, "hoping to establish a legal precedent recognizing the constitutional rights of citizens to a wholesome environment." It has filed suit against the United States Army Corps of Engineers to stop construction of the

our right, and smiling children soon clustered about the plane, eager to help us carry our gear to the lodge.

In recent years Barrantes' lodge at Parismina, and his other, newer establishment forty miles north up the coast on the Colorado River, have produced some of the best tarpon fishing in the world. No giant tarpon (the record is 283 pounds) have been caught at either of these camps, but fish weighing thirty to one hundred pounds are abundant.

The camps are open from January 15 to May 15, during the country's dry season, but this year the weather has been unpredictable. After arriving in San José, Ristori and I learned that torrential rains had just inundated the vast eastern coastal plain.

Rampaging rivers, fed by the innumerable smaller streams draining from the mountains, had torn out bridges, roads, and railway lines and isolated many villagers, with some drownings resulting. Helicopters were used to bring food and medical supplies to isolated communities and to evacuate the sick and injured. It was, according to some reports, the worst flood ever recorded in the area.

The village of Parismina (population about 150) suffered no damage, although flood waters reached some buildings; but the river itself and its tributaries, from the foothills of the mountains to the Caribbean, were chocolate-brown and laden with silt and floating logs and trees when we flew over them.

Barrantes had warned us of the near impossibility of catching tarpon under such conditions, and before flying to Parismina we remained an extra day in San José to visit with Barrantes, his gracious, lovely wife, Louisa, and their children and relatives.

At a family picnic at their country retreat in the La Garita area there was good talk, good food, good rum, and a sensitive and rewarding introduction to the country and its aspirations by the members of this sophisticated, closely knit clan and their friends.

"Tomorrow," Barrantes said as he left us that evening at the Hotel Europa in San José, "we will fly you to Parismina. The river is still high, but perhaps it will soon drop. This is incredible. It never rains at this time."

Baboon Roars As Anglers Catch Tarpon in Costa Rican Lagoon

Parismina, Costa Rica

In the dark recesses of an ever-narrowing lagoon that reached back into the jungle, the blazing tropical sun could no longer reach us, and night shadows came early.

South of us, a mile away, the waves of the Caribbean moaned on miles of lonely beach, and close by, in the towering trees, a male baboon roared pleasure, passion, or discontent.

In the shadows the waters of the lagoon appeared black, and great tarpon were rolling and splashing, sometimes sending a shower of spray three feet into the air.

I hooked a tarpon on an underwater plug, only to have the plug go sailing past me after the fish's first jump.

My companion, Al Ristori of Hackensack, New Jersey, who had already taken a thirty-five-pound tarpon in the Caribbean that morning, said, "There's a hundred-pounder in that pool," and tossed his lure to the spot.

A tarpon hit, jumped, jumped again, and Ristori, noting that the fish was considerably less than one hundred pounds, had the gall to smile and remark, "I'm sorry, he's smaller than I thought."

After six or seven jumps, the tarpon went to the bottom of the pool, which was about twenty-five feet deep and forty yards across at its widest point, and moved in slow circles. This was interesting to a spectator for the first fifteen minutes, but other fish were breaking water all about us, and I was eager to cast to them.

"Put the wood to him," I pleaded, but Ristori already had all pressure possible on his fish. He was using a twenty-pound-test spinning rig.

Night fell, the baboon stopped roaring, the jungle was silent, the big fish continued his slow circles, and our guide turned the boat with him. Eventually Ristori brought him to the surface, but the circling continued. Forty-five minutes after the tarpon first hit, we gaffed him aboard. He was a fifty-four-pounder.

This was our best day of fishing at Carlos Barrantes' tarpon-fishing lodge at Parismina, a tiny village on Costa Rica's east coast.

Torrential rains the previous week had flooded the entire coast, making fishing in the Parismina River impossible. A strong onshore breeze had kept us, for the most part, from fishing the Caribbean itself.

That morning, for perhaps an hour before the wind came up, we had a taste of what tarpon fishing at Parismina can be. A half mile offshore and a mile up the coast from the mouth of the river, we found schools of big tarpon.

Our taciturn guide, Alex Perez, smiled and said, "These tarpon will bite." He was right. They hit everything we threw at them. Lines and leaders parted, plugs and jigs flew through the air as they were tossed back at us by the jumping fish, and when it was all over, Ristori had his thirty-five-pounder.

Ristori lost another larger tarpon, just before it was ready for the gaff, when a big shark chased it to the surface and closed its jaws about the tarpon's midriff. There was a brief flurry, blood stained the water dark brown, and there was a shower of silvery scales.

Barrantes' tarpon camp at Parismina and another north up the coast on the Colorado River offer some of the best tarpon angling in the world from January 15 to May 15 for fish from twenty-five to one hundred pounds. The address of his main office, situated in his sporting goods store, is Gilca Ltda., Apartado 2816, San José, Costa Rica.

Return to New York State's Neversink Is Like Rereading a Classic

Returning after a long winter to a lovely and cherished trout stream in spring's full glory and working it with a fly rod is like rereading a classic: one is astonished and delighted afresh.

Fishing the Neversink in New York State's Catskills with Dr. Bernard Cinberg of Manhattan a few days ago was such an experience.

The silver tarpon of Florida are exciting, as are sailfish, marlins, and broadbill swordfish; moonlit beaches, or the same beaches in the dark of the moon, from which one slings a plug or jig to sea for striped bass are full of mystery and promise, and the striper himself is challenging; a school of bluefish chopping and slashing at silversides on Long Island Sound while screaming terns flash down from above provides thrilling sport; smallmouth bass hitting a popping plug in a shower of bright water can shake a seasoned angler, and the smallmouth is perhaps the hardest-fighting freshwater fish; and the huge shape of a muskellunge sliding under the boat, following the lure after fruitless hours of casting, is almost more than one can bear.

But nothing can match the total discipline, the exquisite delight, of taking a trout on a fly from a stream.

All else pales. Away with your spinning rods, your bait-casting rods, your boat rods and massive saltwater reels, your fighting chairs, your twin screw craft.

On a trout stream the wading fisherman is alone. No skill, save his own—not the guide's skill, nor that of the skipper or the mate, can help him. Fly-fishing is a direct confrontation between man and fish. Before you are the trout, lurking near boulders, hanging in eddies, nymphing in the fast, slick glides at the tail of the pools. How will you entice them?

It is good to be able to throw a long line, say ninety to one hundred feet, but often the long line is not necessary. It is the skill in infighting, the short punch, that counts. See that trout rising from time to time thirty feet away at the edge of the fast water, with the fast water between you and him? It is not enough to drop the fly on his nose; you must present it so it drifts, free of drag, into his vision.

And when fishing a nymph—ah, the patience required; oh, the response a split second too late when you strike after the trout has taken and mouthed and rejected the fly.

Every pool, every pocket, every stretch of fast water on a trout stream is a new problem. Where do you stand? How do you make your presentation? And the trout, whether brook, rainbow, brown, or cutthroat, are as delicately hued as a dewed spiderweb in a dawn meadow, as beautiful as a young dancer, strength and grace exquisitely combined.

Add to this the tradition—the legendary fly-fishermen, European and American, who have over centuries created a literature and technique against which all our efforts are measured—and there is no other conclusion possible: this form of angling, played out on a wild and beautiful stream, surpasses all others.

Chesapeake Bay Stripers Hungry and Numerous, But Not Very Large

Annapolis, Maryland

When we left Gingerville Creek on Cape St. John, a gentle rain was falling and there was not a whisper of wind.

But by the time Don Carpenter of Annapolis was easing his Boston whaler around the treacherous rocks of Thomas Point Light House, wind-driven rain was stinging our faces, and waves rolling from the southeast up Chesapeake Bay were two and a half feet high, with some three-footers thrown in for interest.

Bracing one knee on the seat and a leg against the gunwale, I cast to the rocks around the lighthouse with a fly rod for half an hour, to no avail.

Carpenter put me in all the right places, but the fish weren't there. Before we left we tried casting lures—lures that had been taking fish consistently the past few weeks—but this too failed.

Satisfied that we had given the lighthouse proper attention, we returned to the relative calm of the coves, creeks, and points along the shores of the South River, picking up small stripers in virtually every spot. These were little bass, usually barely exceeding the legal twelve-inch length.

The best lure for them was an oversized shad dart, or jig, basically yellow, with a light tinge of green.

The darts we were using had been made by Clem Wagner of Edgewater, Maryland, Carpenter said. "They've been very effective this year. I usually troll them on about eighty-five feet of monofilament. They should be jigged while trolling," Carpenter added.

A half-hour later another boat trolling the same area proved to be Wagner's. He and John Leatherbury of Deale, Maryland, were fishing together.

We hove to for a gam and admired the fish Leatherbury and Wagner had caught, all larger than ours, averaging perhaps sixteen to eighteen inches.

"Plenty of small ones, but slow going on anything better," said Wagner, who still bore the scars of a recent boating mishap. Flung out of a small outboard-powered skiff while fishing alone in the bay, Wagner had tangled with the propeller when his unmanned skiff made a tight turn and came back over him, cutting his neck and shredding the shoulder of his windbreaker, which he still wears.

Cleaning our stripers at the end of the day, Carpenter remarked that it was too bad we would not have time to try for white American shad in the Potomac River. Carpenter and his wife, Peg, do not limit their eating of the shad to the female's roe. Their recipe calls for rubbing the whole, gutted fish, inside and out, with salt, pepper, and butter, wrapping it in foil, and baking it for six hours at 250 degrees. This, they say, softens all the bones so that the fish may be eaten with ease.

Cape Codder Describes Simple Plan for a Home Smokehouse

Barnstable, Massachusetts

Taisto Ranta, the soft-spoken Finn who is fish and game and beach officer for the town of Barnstable on Cape Cod and who has labored long and diligently to restore the annual spring run of alewives in the Marstons Mills River to its former glory, has what appears to be a splendid idea for a homemade smoking device for alewives and other delicacies of the sea.

Smoked alewives were once an important part of a New Englander's diet, but consumption of locally caught fish is now largely confined to the freshly cooked roe of the female.

Some years ago, Ranta said, a visitor from Alaska had asked why there was so little smoked meat in New England larders. Learning that a lack of proper equipment was often the stumbling block, the man had given Ranta a plan for a simple smoking unit.

Strip the motor and cooling tubing from an old refrigerator (one can usually be found in a town dump), says Ranta, "then get an old hot plate—I use the bottom of a popcorn cooker—and that's all there is to it.

"I fill a large can, I think it's a Number Nine, half full of wood chips, add six paper cups of water, and put it on the hot plate."

Then, he says, all one has to do is hang the brine-soaked alewives, which have been gutted and scaled, in the refrigerator, shut the door, and plug in the hot plate. The fish are done in four hours.

Ranta uses applewood chips, but hickory chips are also good. Chips for smoking are available in certain stores. Obviously, resinous woods, such as pines, would not be good because of their tar content.

Ranta's brine mixture, in which the fish are soaked for eight hours before smoking, calls for three cups of sugar, five to six cups of corning (coarse) salt, a tablespoon of pepper, and a few garlic cloves for each gallon of water.

He hangs the fish from the original refrigerator racks by jamming them head up between the wires of the rack. If, he says, one wishes to hang the fish on individual wires, the wires should not be run through the eye sockets but through the gill plates. If the eye sockets are used, the fish will tear off the wire, he says. Ranta also uses the device for smoking eels. Because smoke and steam leak from the refrigerator, the smoking should not be done in a closed room.

(Certain state and municipal laws require that abandoned refrigerators have their doors removed. The door of a smokehouse refrigerator may be removed when it is not in use, or a chain and padlock may be put around it.)

Delaware River Offers Everything But the Lovely, Shimmering Shad

Narrowsburg, New York

We caught walleyed pike, small-mouth bass, and sunfish, but the lovely, shimmering shad, which run up the river from the ocean each spring to spawn, eluded us in a day and a half of fishing on the Delaware River.

Accompanied by Joe Purcell, a master mariner who gave up the sea and returned to Narrowsburg for a life on land, Zack Taylor of Fair Haven, New Jersey, and I worked diligently up and down the river near Narrowsburg, sustained by stories of nice shad having been taken in the area a few days before.

The basic lure for shad is a small bucktail jig thrown with either a spinning rod or conventional bait-casting gear. The jigs Purcell provided us with were yellow and white. Spotting the jigs that adorned Purcell's fishing cap, one unidentified fisherman in the Century Hotel in Narrowsburg informed us that he and his friends had caught several large shad the day before, but, he added, "Forget the white jigs. Only the yellow. They wouldn't touch the white."

We thanked him for his information, feeling reasonably certain that our white and yellow lures were a workable compromise.

Purcell, who is a dedicated hunter and fisherman and conservationist, is Parks and Recreation Administrator for Sullivan County, a Sullivan County planning director, and a member of the Delaware-Sullivan Counties Water Resources Commission.

Purcell is in love with the upper Delaware, and it is easy to see why. Its waters are clear, and there is very little shore development. It holds in season, despite our inability to catch them, good runs of shad, as well as smallmouth bass, walleyes, pickerel, and rainbow and brown trout.

Although Taylor, who is an editor for *Sports Afield* magazine, and I caught no shad—we blamed it on the water temperature, which was a cool 55 degrees—we both began making plans for a return visit and a float trip.

Any section of the Delaware, say from Hancock to Port Jervis, is ideally suited for such an excursion. There are several public and private lunching areas and a good number of campsites. A float trip in June or July would result in some fine smallmouth bass fishing. One could either camp at various spots along the river or put in at any of the shoresite communities, which have fine restaurants and hotels and motels. (Ten recreation maps of the nontidal Delaware may be obtained for one dollar from the Delaware River Basin Commission, 23 Scotch Road, Suburban Square, Trenton, New Jersey.)

As Purcell points out, it is rather astonishing that a river within two hours drive of New York City's millions has remained virtually unspoiled. And, he adds, "There is probably not another river in the Northeast of its size that has such excellent water quality." He is pleased that the stream is under study for possible protection under the National Scenic Rivers legislation.

Cape Cod Trout Ponds Are Excellent and Often Neglected in Summer and Fall

Barnstable, Massachusetts

A newly arrived young man with a spinning rod baited his hook with one orange salmon egg and casually flipped it into the wind-ruffled waters of Hamblin Pond.

Five minutes later he had a fat fifteen-inch brown trout. He gutted the fish expertly and also cut out its gills, approved procedure for keeping a trout fit for the table, then fastened it to a stringer and dropped it into the water, thereby tarnishing the image of expertness that he was creating. Dead fish spoil more rapidly in water than in air. In all fairness, however, he could have argued that the pond was still cold enough to warrant his act; the water probably was somewhere between 50 and 55 degrees.

It was, I believe, the cold water that forced me to work much harder for my first fish, a thirteen-inch brown, which finally hit after five hours of fly-casting.

In perhaps another two weeks Hamblin will be in top shape for the fly-fishermen. There were some sporadic hatches of small aquatic insects today, confined for the most part to the early evening. During the day an occasional trout rose (there may have been more but they were hard to spot because of the choppy water), and just before sunset many small fish were surface-feeding along the east shore of the pond.

Four of these little fellows, about seven inches long, took a small gray nymph I offered them, and all were returned to the water.

Hamblin, which covers 149 acres, is one of the better Cape Cod trout ponds that are available for public fishing. Most can be worked fairly easily by a fly-fisherman wearing waders. The fishing pressure can be fairly intense when the season opens late in April and for a few weeks thereafter, but soon the lure of the sea calls many of these anglers away.

The first striped bass has already been caught at Popponesset on the Cape, and by the middle of this month they should be present in great numbers. Spring flounder fishing is in full swing. Late in April two eight-year-old boys, Eric Scherer of Chatham and Mark Hammond of East Harwich, caught seventy-five flounders in Pleasant Bay in a single day. Bluefish will show late in June or early in July.

Those fishing the Cape's trout waters for the first time would do well to obtain the *Sportsman's Guide to Cape Cod,* published, in cooperation with the Massachusetts Division of Fisheries and Game, by the Cape Cod Chamber of Commerce in Hyannis.

This brochure, one side of which is a map of the Cape, lists pond and stream fishing locations, boat launching sites, and boat liveries. It also indicates surf-fishing access routes and saltwater launching sites.

Detailed maps of the ponds themselves may be obtained by sending a stamped, addressed envelope to the Information Education Section, Fisheries and Game Field Headquarters, Westboro, Massachusetts. The limit is five maps per person.

Of course, finding a pond is one thing and learning to fish it another. One could work a trout pond every day of the season for two years and still not know all the answers.

Pickerel Provide Exciting Action When Offered Fly-Rod Popping Plugs

West Tisbury, Massachusetts

A small green-and-gold pickerel danced halfway across the cove in pursuit of a minnow, traveling two feet in the air and two feet in the water alternately.

A pair of wood ducks scrambled out of the swamp at the head of the cove and flew directly over our heads, conversing nervously. High above, from his broad circle in the bright spring air a hawk sounded a thin metallic cry, and from swaying bushes red-winged blackbirds sang of the land's awakening.

My brother Dan and I had come to this freshwater pond, one of several tucked behind the beaches on the south shore of Martha's Vineyard Island, to determine whether pickerel could be consistently caught with a fly rod and a popping plug.

Pickerel are not great fighters, but they do provide good sport on light tackle. Live minnows, or plugs and spoons, thrown with either spinning or conventional bait-casting gear, are the usual equipment one uses on pickerel. A quarter of a century ago a common pickerel-fishing technique was to skitter a pork rind strip through the shallows with a twelve- or fourteen-foot cane pole, but this is rarely seen today.

More than a decade ago I discovered that pickerel fishing, with a fly rod and streamer flies, was a good way to find action in the East after the close of the trout season in early fall, but I had never tried popping plugs.

In two hours of late afternoon fishing, Dan and I caught ten pickerel on poppers ranging from twenty to twenty-two inches long, releasing all but three.

From time to time, to test the efficacy of the poppers, I switched to streamer flies but could not attract a fish. The plugs we used were large, designed for striped bass. Red and white and green and white combinations were effective. The water we fished was shallow, from three to six feet, and one of the pleasures of using the top-water plug was that we could often see the wake of the fish as he hurtled toward the lure.

During the time we fished, two other anglers, using spinning rods and small spoons, were working the same area. They took no fish.

A brisk southeast breeze that had been blowing all day died with the setting of the sun, and a pale moon, almost perfectly round, lifted above the oak forest to the east. A pair of blue-winged teal sideslipped over the cove and landed a few yards from us. The sky was still diffused with red when two Canadian geese came low out of the west. They communicated with each other as they flew and cried to all on the pond to see if any others of their species were about. They passed directly over our heads, twenty-five yards away, and did not see us until we lifted our fly rods in salute.

On the way back to the car I picked a handful of young cattail shoots (I like them boiled in salted water with a strip of bacon thrown in), but passed up a clump of fiddlehead ferns because I have never found a quick way to remove the bitter, fuzzy outer covering.

Timber Wolf Gaining Backers in Alaska, His Last Stronghold

In Alaska, his last stronghold in the United States, the timber wolf is no longer regarded with unmitigated loathing by the general public.

Speaking to the recent North American Wildlife and Natural Resources conference in Washington, Robert A. Rausche of the Alaska Department of Fish and Game said that the state legislature's passage of two bills last year indicated "a considerable change in attitude [toward wolves] in the past fifteen years."

The laws prohibit the poisoning of wolves without written permission from the Fish and Game Board and place all authorization for bounties on wolves, wolverines, and coyotes within the board's jurisdiction.

In addition, he said, the state senate considered a bill that would have outlawed hunting from aircraft, a common technique for killing wolves. Even the consideration of such a measure would not have been possible a decade ago, he implied.

By 1925 the timber wolf had almost been eradicated from the forty-eight states, but in the intervening years there has been a growing feeling on the part of fish and game departments, conservationists, and the general public that predators such as wolves have a role in the natural scheme and that their presence is not detrimental to other wildlife.

In the United States, only Alaska now has a substantial population of timber wolves. There are a few in the northern parts of Minnesota, Wisconsin, and Michigan, and they are protected in those states. Timber wolves are fairly numerous in Canada and range northward into Greenland.

A full-grown timber wolf, also known as a gray wolf, may weigh more than one hundred pounds and stand three feet high at the shoulder.

Rausche told of a ten-year study of timber wolves in the Nelchina Basin caribou range and adjoining areas, covering twenty thousand square miles in south-central Alaska. At the start of the study in 1957 fewer than twenty wolves were in the area. Under protection they increased to a high of 450 in 1965.

By last year, when they were no longer protected, their number had dropped to three hundred. There were various reasons, according to Rausche, including poaching, hard winters, and the wolves' pursuit of caribou, one of their prime sources of food, into an unprotected area.

Studies of the contents of Nelchina wolves' stomachs showed that moose was their favorite ungulate (hooved) prey, followed by caribou. Dall sheep were also eaten. A rough estimate of the number of caribou in the area was sixty-six thousand; for moose the estimate was twenty-five thousand.

Rausche said that there was no evidence to suggest that the growing wolf population had any significant adverse effect on the caribou or moose.

Because cattle and other domestic animals are not in the area, there is no problem involving the killing of stock by wolves, Rausche said; but, he added, some hunters feel that the wolf represents competition for such game species as caribou, moose, and Dall sheep.

But, citing the previously mentioned laws, he said there was a strong indication that the bounties on wolves, coyotes, and wolverines would be lifted in selected areas of the state.

(This column was published in March, 1969.)

Does a Tree Scream Silently When an Ax Bites into It?

$\mathbf{I}$t is possible that a giant oak quails when a burly woodsman approaches it with an ax, or grows apprehensive when a fox kills a rabbit nearby.

This is one interpretation of information in an article in the February–March issue of *National Wildlife* magazine, in which its author, Thorn Bacon, explores some of the work done by Cleve Backster of the Backster Research Foundation in New York City. Backster, described as a "former interrogation specialist with the Central Intelligence Agency," trains police officers in the use of the polygraph, or lie detector.

Two years ago Backster attached electrodes to the leaves of a plant, intending to measure, through psychogalvanic reflex (PGR), the rate of moisture ascent in the plant following watering.

Eventually wondering whether the plant's PGR tracing (on a graph) would show any reaction when the plant was exposed to stress, he dunked a leaf in hot coffee. There was no measurable reaction. Later, casting about for a greater threat, he decided to burn the leaf being tested with a match. At the moment of his thought, the PGR tracing indicated what would have been interpreted as emotional stress in a human.

Backster also found that his plants reacted violently (on the PGR tracing) when he dropped live shrimp in boiling water. He now wonders, according to the article, if when a living cell dies, it signals that death to other living cells.

Looking at the simpler rather than the profound implications of Backster's work, it is now clear why some people have a green thumb and some do not, why tomatoes flourish in one garden and languish in another. If the gardener approaches his plants and their entourage of bugs, barn grass, and weeds with irritation, he may do more harm than good. Picture a row of green beans shrinking in terror at a flailing hoe in the hands of a man who would rather be wielding a golf club. Several such experiences would surely stunt them.

It is clear that if one cannot enter a garden overflowing with love and happy sounds, no seeds should be sown.

Backster's discovery also offers a chance for undercover work by rival gardeners. If your neighbor's strawberries are getting ahead of yours, sneak out to his plot in the full of the moon and think evil thoughts.

(This column was published in March, 1969.)

Summer

Not All My Dreams Are Lost;
I Could Create a Classic Fly

$\mathbf{O}$nce I wanted to write a great lyric poem, make a million dollars, and own the island of Naushon.

Now I will settle for a decent sonnet, something less than a million, and an occasional stroll on Naushon's beaches.

This is not defeatism, just logic. Most lyric poets are running downhill after thirty. Admittedly, making a million, or millions, can come late in life: Colonel Sanders and his chickens have proved that. But after more than a quarter of a century of working for wages I have learned that I have no nose for money, and Naushon has remained lovely and unspoiled without my help.

One of my lesser goals, to create a classic trout fly, is still within reach, however.

Anyone can tie a fly and name it after himself, but the trick is to create one that will be used consistently by other fishermen. For this reason it should also be attractive to fish.

Over the years I have labored at my fly-tying labors long after the rest of the house is asleep, trying to find that one classic fly. Many of my inventions were little more than variations on existing patterns, and all of them took fish. Only one of my own patterns failed utterly. It was made from fibers stolen from a cherished whiskbroom that had belonged to my mother's grandmother. I cannot take a fish with it, nor can I lose it. It rests secure in my fly book, a constant reminder of my youthful indiscretion.

Ten years ago I developed an interesting little nymph that may be the answer. It is made from hairs clipped from my chest and I've had fair success with it. I shall try tying a few more of these soon, for some of the hair is grey now and the new color scheme may make the difference between mediocrity and brilliance.

I could call it 46-47 (46 for chest inches, 47 for years). The next step would be to give a few to some of my trout-fishing friends, preferably those who talk a great deal or who write for newspapers or outdoor publications.

Just a few mentions here and there could turn the tide. Something like, "My day on the Battenkill was a disaster until I tied on Bryant's exquisite little nymph, the 46-47," or, "The ten-pound brown in Balderdash Pool, a fish that had refused all offerings throughout the summer, took my 46-47 with a tremendous rush, his gold sides gleaming in the last light of evening."

These flies would, for obvious reasons, be limited in number, ideal gifts for close friends or heads of state. I would, if my calculations are correct, be able to produce six dozen a year without venturing off prime territory, and would, of course, always set aside a tuft or two for emergencies and gallant gestures.

Picture Lady Lightcreel distraught in her coracle, trout rising all about her, and her gillie wringing his hands because she has just snapped off her last 46-47 on a big Loch Leven. Picture me tearing open my windbreaker, wrenching the necessary materials from my bosom, and fashioning a fly on the spot.

That's the stuff from which legends are made.

Fly-Fishermen Fail
to Catch Many
Long Island Blues, Stripers

Shelter Island, Long Island

A stiff breeze that slanted against Hay Beach from the east failed to die, as it often does along the seacoast at sunset, making it difficult to cast our big saltwater streamers.

We were participating in the recent annual meeting of Metropolitan Chapter 6, Salt Water Fly Rodders of America, at Shelter Island. Nestled between the two western prongs of Long Island and accessible by ferry from Greenport and South Haven, sparsely populated Shelter Island, although only one hundred miles from New York City, is a lovely spot, much of it heavily wooded and untarnished by haphazard or tasteless residential and commercial development.

Setting forth from the Dering Harbor Motel in late afternoons and before dawn, more than fifty eastern fly-rod anglers strove mightily to catch striped bass and bluefish, but the nagging wind and an unfortunate scarcity of the species limited the total bagged to a few dozen fish, most of them blues. Many were caught from boats and many were taken, although one hesitates to admit it, with plebeian spinning tackle. One good-sized striper, a twenty-two-pounder, was caught on spinning gear and a plug the second evening.

A few anglers eschewed all pretense at total devotion to fly-rod fishing and went forth with bait to pluck porgies (scup) and flounders from the bottom.

The organizer of the affair, Dom DeSalvo of Elmhurst, Queens, president of Chapter 6, expressed chagrin over the mediocre fishing —it had been very good a little more than a week before—but many assembled anglers took pains to assure him that the beauty of the place more than compensated for the uncooperative fish.

With its many miles of shoreline indented by coves and harbors, Shelter Island is ideal for saltwater fly-fishermen when fish are hitting. Really large blues (over ten pounds) or stripers (over thirty) are rare, but from spring into late fall there is usually excellent angling for smaller representatives of both species.

The specialized art of fly-fishing in salt water has gained immensely in popularity during the last decade. One of the founders of the Salt Water Fly Rodders of America, Elwood Colvin of Seaside Park, New Jersey, was present at the Shelter Island meeting. Colvin and many of the various chapter members are so dedicated to the fly rod that they will not resort to spinning or conventional tackle even when conditions virtually demand it.

To a man, the contingent from Rhode Island, the Rhody Fly Rodders, were of this persuasion. After meeting four of them on the New London–Orient Point Long Island ferry, I cast my lot with this group of friendly anglers, who included Albert Brewster and his son, Ernest, of Riverside, Edward Ward of Cumberland, Tom Camara of Warwick, Elmer Fogg of Rumford, and Carl Bruscini and Ronald Montecalvo, both of Providence.

Surf-Casting at Night
a Strange and
Moving Experience

West Tisbury, Massachusetts

The night was black, and a cold rain rode on the east wind. It was so dark that only the white water of the surf could be seen faintly, except when lightning flickered in the west, illuminating broken waves and tumbling water. From time to time floating planks and other debris nearly knocked me off my feet as I stood knee-deep in the wash.

The striped bass were there, but were hitting indifferently. They had moved along the south shore of Martha's Vineyard Island searching for food and had found the bait-laden outrunning waters of Tisbury Great Pond recently opened to the sea. The previous night my brother Dan had taken six fish averaging better than twenty pounds each, but I could not duplicate his success. Three times in a dozen casts a fish took my plug, a big underwater Atom, and each time made a short run before breaking free. My brother had the same experience, then managed to beach one that weighed about eighteen pounds.

His lure was also the large underwater Atom.

"I use nothing else off the beach after dark," he said, and after experimenting with different lures for an hour, I gave credence to his theory, at least on that particular evening.

To many saltwater fishermen, surf-casting at night is the ultimate in angling pleasure. Its attractions are many. It is good to have solid ground underfoot, rather than the heaving deck of a boat, and solitude can usually be had, if desired, by walking a few hundred yards down the beach.

Dark nights seem to produce the best fishing, although I have taken stripers when the moon was full and the fins of the fish could be seen cutting through shallow water as they pursued the lure. There is a general inshore movement of large fish after dark. They are chasing bait fish that seek sanctuary in the shallows.

During the daylight hours this is a reasonably effective maneuver for the little ones, but at night, particularly on a flood tide, striped bass and other predatory fish often move inshore until they are a few feet off the beach. The smaller fish are often driven out of water onto land by their pursuers at such a time.

Surf-fishing after sunset can be a strange and moving experience. If the night is black, one casts into a void, and when a fish hits and stays on, there is often a sensation that one is connected by a fragile and singing line to the source of all life.

But even as the mystic experience is under way, the experienced angler is taking note of the behavior of the fish and guessing at his size and identity. Stripers, for example, usually make one long run before settling down to a series of shorter, dogged rushes. Bluefish, on the other hand, usually fight a distinguished battle all the way.

And if the fish is brought ashore under the moon, one may recall that some old-time New England beach fishermen believed moonlight spoiled the flesh of a fish. They would promptly bury their catch in the sand to protect it from the lunar glow. This burying ritual is still practiced by old-timers today, but the motive is to hide their success from those who pass by rather than a fear of moonsickness.

Drain Plunger Flushes Clams from Their Lair without Harm

Chilmark, Massachusetts

Ever since an intrepid aborigine first hauled several soft-shell clams out of the muck of a tidal flat, laid them on the coals of his cooking fire to stew in their own juices, and found them good, his descendants have striven to devise a quick and easy way to harvest the tasty bivalves.

Some clams, the hard-shelled quahog for example, rest with a portion of their shell above the sand. Thus they are visible to the gatherer and may be easily plucked from the bottom, or if the water is murky they may be found by treading over the bottom barefoot or by using a special quahog rake.

The wily steamer, or soft-shell clam, hides several inches beneath the bottom, maintaining contact with the sea above through his long neck.

The usual way to get steamers is to dig with one's hands in the shallow water on a mud flat above the telltale holes that mean clams are below.

The hand-digging method has one major drawback, particularly for women who care about the condition of their hands. The muck in which the clams hide is usually loaded with small bits of shells. The invariable result is broken fingernails and cut fingers.

Various tools, including spades, forks, shovels, and hoes, may be used to dig clams. Their primary drawback is that many of the fragile shells are broken in the process.

The origin of the first major breakthrough in amateur clam-digging techniques is not known, although there are some residents of remote Cuttyhunk Island, off the Massachusetts coast, who say it began there. The tool is the common drain plunger. This ubiquitous household object, when agitated forcefully on an underwater clam bed, brings the creatures out of their lairs in a swirling caldron of water. There is no damage to clams or fingernails, and a plunger will last the average family several seasons.

Some plunger devotees advocate making a large circular hole in the clam bed; others hold out for the trench. It's all a matter of individual preference. One can tell when the clams are being uprooted, for they can be spotted as they swirl momentarily to the surface in the muddy whirlpool around the plunger before sinking to the bottom. After making the hole or trench, allow the water to clear and then gather the clams that will be resting on the newly plowed bottom like so many potatoes.

Although the classic fate of the soft-shell clam is the clambake or steaming pot, it does make an excellent chowder.

Procure enough clams to provide about two and a half cups of clam meats (this could be as many as ten dozen small clams) and steam them open. Remove the meats from the shells, skinning the necks in the process, and save a quart of the clam broth.

Dice fine a quarter of a pound of salt pork and brown it in a large pot. Dice fine two medium-sized potatoes and two medium-sized carrots and add the vegetables to the pot along with the clam broth, plus a one-pound can of whole tomatoes.

When the vegetables are almost done add a few sprigs of parsley, and when the cooking is over toss in the clam meats. Salt and pepper to taste afterward. This is an adequate amount for a family of five.

Visit to Noman's Land Island Produces Harvest of Giant Blues

Edward "Spider" Andresen and I were headed for Noman's Land Island in his twenty-four-foot Wahoo when we saw herring gulls hovering over Devil's Bridge, a nasty underwater rock ledge off Gay Head on Martha's Vineyard Island.

Moving in closer, we saw breaking fish. They were small bluefish, three to five pounds, pursuing schools of baby herring.

"Should we stop?" asked Spider. Our goal at Noman's was bluefish up to eighteen pounds that had been there since early summer.

We hesitated for a moment only. Then, with breaking fish all around us, we unlimbered our rods and began casting.

The blues hit white popping plugs freely, and we soon had a dozen in the boat. Switching from a spinning rod to a fly rod, I caught half a dozen blues on an all-pink streamer fly designed for tarpon and a striped bass fly rod popping plug. Long casts were not necessary. The blues were often twenty feet from the boat. I lost a few flies and the plug when the blues chopped through my twelve-pound-test tippet. Adding eight inches of fine wire leader, I had no further trouble.

When using large saltwater plugs or jigs for blues, one may safely attach the lure directly to the spinning or casting line, but blues frequently engulf a fly and in so doing cut the leader. The aforementioned short, light wire leader avoids this, and some saltwater fly rodders substitute a so-called shock tippet of heavy monofilament, forty or sixty pound test, or heavier, for the wire.

We also took two striped bass of ten and twenty-three pounds by fishing deep running plugs under the surface-feeding bluefish.

The best was yet to come, however. Running to Noman's we put Andresen's boat, the *Sarah D.*, among the rocks about seventy yards from the beach on the back side of the island, and virtually every cast with spinning gear and poppers had us fast to blues that ranged from eight to eighteen pounds.

It was not possible, because of the heavy swells and dangerous rocks, to get within fly-casting distance of these big fish, although we had hoped to do so.

In an hour and a half of furious action there were many times, with two fish fast, when one of us had to run the boat with one hand and fight the fish with the other. It was not a place for the inexpert or timorous boatman or fisherman. Jagged rocks rose streaming from the surge or loomed dark a few feet below the surface. (A few days after our trip a fisherman friend of Andrcsen's lost his boat in the same spot.)

Seaward of us, half a dozen boats worked the deeper water and picked up an occasional blue by trolling.

The fish box overflowing, we pulled out and began the forty-minute run back to the dock at Menemsha Marine, where Andresen bases his charter boat business.

Shooting a Well Brings Psychic Release, and Sometimes Good Water

Nelson," said Luciano Rebay over the telephone, "I remember that last year you said you would like to shoot my well. Would you still like to do it?"

"I'd be delighted," I replied. "I'll be over tomorrow."

Rebay, who is professor of Italian at Columbia University and who summers with his family in Lambert's Cove on Martha's Vineyard, was pleased. "It is taking from forty-five minutes to an hour to fill the tank now, so something has to be done. I recall that you said shooting a well is a last resort. We have, I think, reached that stage."

Most Vineyard residents get their water from shallow wells, one-and-one-quarter-inch pipes driven into the earth until they penetrate the water table. A well point is at the lower end of the pipe. The usual well point is three or four feet long with a cone-shaped end, and is perforated with holes covered with bronze screening. The screening allows the water to enter the pipe, but holds sand or clay out.

Under normal conditions the screens, or "buttons," on the well point holes begin to clog with debris after two years or more, and the pump labors to fill the water tank. Eventually the buttons get clogged so badly that the pipe must be pulled and the point replaced. Before the final and expensive step of pulling the point is taken, one may shoot his well.

The unsung hero who first thought of shooting a well is lost to history, but the technique lives on. Shooting a well often gives a homeowner another two or three years of water, and if it fails nothing is lost. Shooting a well is also a good way to work off repressed violence. After fighting a balky water system for weeks, it is eminently satisfying to shoot it. The proper weapon for wells is the .22 long rifle rimfire. One unscrews the cap on the vertical well pipe, and with a companion standing back to "eyeball" the rifle, thus making sure it is aligned with the pipe, fires one, two, or three rounds down into the water in the pipe. If all goes well, the shock of the bullets striking the water blows the debris off the buttons.

Sometimes the shock blows the buttons right out of the point. If this happens, the point must be replaced. For this reason, a larger caliber than the .22 is not recommended. Some angry souls have used .410-gauge shotguns with rifled slugs, but this often blows the buttons.

After giving his well three shots, Rebay and I struggled for an hour to get his pump primed, then retired in disgust to his kitchen, where with his charming wife, Martha, we discussed poetry peripherally and wells centrally.

I was disconsolate, feeling that I had made things worse, but an hour later Rebay went to his cellar, prepared, as he put it, to attack the entire water system, and flipped the switch on the pump, which promptly responded by filling the tank in five minutes.

Shooting wells is not confined to the Vineyard. During a muskellunge fishing trip in Minnesota two years ago, I met a resort owner who told me he had successfully shot his well two days before.

Live Alewives Superior Bait for Striped Bass in the Spring

Persistence is nearly as valuable as skill to an angler, and he usually does not have the latter without the former.

And persistence, while it does not always produce fish, does provide a pleasant by-product: the opportunity to observe wind, weather, tides, fish, and birds over a prolonged period. Such was a recent eight-hour stint on Menemsha Pond on Martha's Vineyard Island.

At sunset there were fifteen of us standing waist-deep in the pond, heaving out live alewives and waiting for striped bass to hit.

The night was dark until the moon rose, three-quarters full and half obscured by a dark cloud.

The water pulsated with life: hundreds of thousands of alewives making their spawning run up Herring Creek to Squibnocket Pond. (On the creek itself is the works where the fish are netted commercially by Lorenzo Jeffers of Gay Head and Mashpee, Massachusetts, a sachem of the Wampanoag Indian tribe. One should, before fishing the area, obtain permission to do so from Jeffers.)

By 10 P.M. eight of us remained, and three or four stripers had been caught, one weighing about fifteen pounds. The alewives continued to mill about the mouth of the creek, making occasional surges up it. When the moon rose higher they remained farther offshore, and by midnight, when the moon was near its meridian, the spawning fish scattered and it became difficult to snag a fresh bait. (The alewives are snagged with a large treble hook cast into their midst.)

When fishing for stripers with live alewives, one leaves the line free so it can spin off the reel without drag, for the bass must have time to swallow the bait. Stripers take the alewife at top speed, and the line flows rapidly from the reel. If an angler strikes too soon he will reel in a bare hook or a hook with a dead alewife on it. The alewife will usually not be cut in any way (stripers don't have cutting teeth), but it will be dead and partially denuded of its scales.

Dogfish also pursue the alewives, and a hooked alewife hit by a dogfish will lack head or tail or both, or will have cleanly cut crescent-shaped chunks taken from its body.

By 3 A.M. only two of us were left. The moon completed its low, southern arc, darkness returned, and the alewives, no longer having the light to fear, moved in, leaping, splashing, and bumping against our waders. A pair of black ducks, identified by their gabble, flew overhead, unseen; whippoorwills sang from the hills; and once the cry of a Canada goose came down the night sky. By then I had caught one striper, a ten-pounder, lost four, and caught four dogfish.

At three thirty my companion, who wore a red hooded sweatshirt, left the water with two stripers. I fished until four, losing one more bass, snagged a dozen female alewives (their roe, fried in butter, would be my breakfast), and departed, having, I thought, outlasted everyone. But Red Sweatshirt's car was still parked on the bluff, and when I walked by he popped up from his nap on the front seat and announced that he was going back for more.

Scrappy Ouananiche Abound in Remote Quebec Lake

Musquaro Lake, Quebec

There is a small but brawling stream that rushes out into the northeastern edge of this remote wilderness lake, forming a pool where brook trout and ouananiche (landlocked salmon) rest and feed.

It is a lovely spot, strewn with large boulders and framed by conifers that line the edge of the stream and reach back into the hills.

From the pool I took eight ouananiche, the largest three pounds, and an equal number of brook trout, some weighing more than a pound.

With our guide, Armand Jenniss, William Fripp of Cambridge, Massachusetts, and I fished this pool for two hours. We were guests of the St. Lawrence Hunting and Fishing Club at the club's Musquaro Lake camp, one of eight wilderness facilities in eastern Quebec operated by the club and accessible only by float plane.

When we reached the pool and anchored our canoe, a sleek dark-brown head rose from the water beside us—an otter hunting for his noon meal. He dived deep into the pool, and several trout leaped out of the water before him.

We tried streamer flies and spinning lures for half an hour with no success. Then I switched to a yellow nymph on a small No. 12 hook. This, used with a sinking line, proved effective on both ouananiche and trout.

Later in the day Jenniss took us to a cove not far from camp where, he predicted, the fishing would be good. That afternoon and the following morning we took many fish from Jenniss' location. Some fell victim to Fripp's trolled streamer, which was just under the water on a floating fly line. Others hit spinning lures and large streamers fished deep.

Until dusk a big yellow streamer fastened to a medium-sized Kastmaster jig was remarkably effective. Later a red Alou bait tail in quarter- and half-ounce sizes sometimes brought a dozen strikes in less than a minute.

This Alou lure was also good when bright sunlight was on the water, but we soon learned that it had to be adapted for trout and ouananiche angling.

It carries a single hook set about halfway back on the plastic body, and many of the fish escape capture by hitting the tail behind the hook. I hastily jury-rigged a tail hook on one of these lures and eliminated the problem.

Another excellent lure for Musquaro trout and salmon is the red and white Dardevle spoon.

At one time or another the fish took a wide variety of lures and many different flies, and the flies ranged from small nymphs to striped bass bucktails on large hooks. I took a two-and-three-quarter-pound brook trout with a large yellow striped bass fly. Another trout, slightly larger, showed a remarkable lack of sophistication: Fripp was playing a one-pound trout on his light fly rod and the big fellow rose in pursuit, evidently sensing an easy meal. I dangled a Kastmaster in front of him, and after hitting it twice and escaping, he took it a third time and was hooked and boated.

Grilled Ouananiche on Lake Shore Delight Anglers Who Caught Them

Musquaro Lake, Quebec

This is a lovely land, a wild land, a land of conifers, lakes, streams, caribou, bears, deer, and the hard-fighting ouananiche, or landlocked salmon.

It is also a land of giant brook trout (some call him the speckled trout or squaretail), reaching eight pounds and more.

Lounging on a rock outcropping on the northwest shore of the lake, our party of seven watched the guides prepare several of the red-fleshed ouananiche for lunch. The fish were split down one side of the backbone, with the skin of the belly holding the two halves together, then laid flat on a wire grill.

Led by a bush pilot, Ronald Ferguson, a man of many talents, the three guides dusted the fish with salt and pepper, covered them with a light layer of brown sugar, then wired another grill over the top of them. Using wires fastened to the grill, two men held the fish suspended over glowing coals of dead juniper, a procedure that guaranteed the proper amount of heat at all times.

With the fish we had hot tea, fresh tomatoes, and homemade bread baked the day before at the camp by Ethel Court, wife of guide John Court.

Contentment was on every face during that lunch hour. The fish-

90

ing had been amazingly good, with dozens of ouananiche up to four pounds having been caught. Many were, of course, released. And among them were several brook trout, some weighing about a pound, and one going over three pounds.

No one was more content than our host, Gordon W. Blair of Huntingdon Valley, Pennsylvania. Blair is financial vice president of Crown Cork & Seal Company, Inc., and founder of the St. Lawrence Hunting and Fishing Club.

Musquaro Lake is one of eight wilderness locations in eastern Quebec at which the club maintains remarkably comfortable bush camps accessible only by airplane and complete with running water, refrigeration, flush toilets, and bed linen. The club leases exclusive fishing rights on the lakes from the Quebec government.

At these camps all a man or a woman has to do is fish or hunt. The fishing season runs from June 1 to September 15. Hunting for caribou is in September. Information on rates and reservations may be obtained by writing the club at 245 Welsh Road, Huntingdon Valley, Pennsylvania 19006.

The caribou hunting is on a par with the fishing. In the last two seasons (since caribou hunting was opened to the public) forty-six of the club's forty-eight hunting guests shot caribou. The remaining two missed their shots.

We caught no large ouananiche, but Jim Hausman of Garden City, Long Island, got a jump or two out of one ouananiche that was estimated at ten to fifteen pounds.

Both trout and ouananiche responded to spoons and jigs on spinning gear and flies and nymphs on fly rods. The best all-around fly, according to the guides, is one that resembles a Mickey Finn. A sinking line was needed when fly-casting, but in another few weeks the fish will also be surface-feeding.

Narragansett Bay's Art Lavallee Knows How to Find Bluefish

Warwick, Rhode Island

Jouncing in three-foot waves in six feet of water off Prudence Island in Narragansett Bay, Art Lavallee's outboard launch performed ably as we flung our plugs down the moaning wind.

Bluefish, coursing up and down a few yards off the beach, were between us and the foam-flecked shore, and occasionally one of them would spot a lure in the wild water and make a pass at it.

It was sunset, but the sun could not be seen. An ominous blackness covered the entire sky from the southeast to the southwest, and we could not refrain from glancing over our shoulders at it from time to time.

In an hour we caught four blues, two about six pounds, two smaller, and one seven-pound striped bass. We lost at least twice that number of fish, and the reason for this may have been the rough water. Our surface plugs were in the air half the time as we retrieved them through the waves, making it difficult for the fish to see or connect with them.

At such a time it is often wise to cast parallel to the waves when using surface plugs, working the lure through the troughs of the waves. This is, of course, no good if the fish are directly downwind or upwind.

A trip on the bay with Lavallee is always pleasurable, for in addition to being a good fisherman with a thorough knowledge of the area, he is also a splendid companion. His fondness for fishing dovetails nicely with one of his businesses, the Acme Tackle Company of Providence, Rhode Island, whose best-known lure is the Kastmaster, a plated jig cut out of round bars of marine brass that has proved effective on everything from trout to striped bass.

Lavallee's firm also makes another lure, a plastic surface plug named the Proper Poppa, for stripers and blues. He has apparently trained Prudence Island fish to respond only to this lure, for it alone caught fish that windy evening. I tried five or six other plugs, swimmers and poppers, made by different manufacturers, with no success. It was Proper Poppa day at Prudence Island, a fact Lavallee noted with glee as we pounded home in the darkness to Earl Steere's Warwick Cove Marina.

School stripers were first caught at Narragansett Bay near the end of April, and fish up to forty pounds have been caught since May 20. Most of the large stripers have hit live alewives, but when the alewives end their spawning run, which will be soon, the big fish will begin paying more attention to artificial lures.

Bluefish running from two to eight pounds moved into the bay May 26. A major part of their present diet is squid.

Narragansett Bay fishing is often "blind," that is to say, there are no visible signs of blues, bass, bait, or birds. One must, through experience, know where the fish will be. One rule Lavallee advances for bluefishing in the bay is that there should be a southerly wind and a high tide.

Chappaquiddick Island Bluefish Find Popping Plugs Enticing

Chappaquiddick Island, Massachusetts

It was late afternoon, a gentle wind came out of the south, and small waves barely rattled the pebbles on the shore.

Before us Nantucket Sound was smooth, so smooth we could see the fins of large bluefish as they cruised back and forth more than a hundred yards offshore. Often a dozen or more of the fish moved in unison, pushing a low wall of water before them.

The East Beach of Chappaquiddick, where we were fishing, is known as a popping-plug beach. The blues in that location do not often want anything else, and this proved true once again. A large all-white popping plug was the proper medicine, and two of us took six fish, up to twelve and a half pounds, in two hours.

The fishing was slow if measured against the number of fish present. Only once did a squadron of the blues react with their normal ferocity, and at that time we both had a fish on. Most of the time a plug drawn through a school would elicit one or two boils or a halfhearted strike. We tried a variety of lures, including swimming plugs, metal jigs, and plastic eels, but the large popper caught all the fish.

As is often the case on East Beach, there were no birds, herring gulls, or terns present. The angling in this location is usually blind, and it was only the combination of flat water and surface-running fish that allowed us to see our prey.

Fast to my first blue, a ten-pounder, I was once again reminded that there is probably no harder-fighting fish in the ocean. Although my surf rod carried twenty-pound-test monofilament, it took fully five minutes to beach the fish. And I was putting a great deal of pressure on because a school had moved close to shore and I wanted to get my lure back in the water as soon as possible.

Big bluefish—any blue over ten pounds may be considered large —have been off Chappaquiddick for more than a week. If they follow their usual summer pattern, they should soon show up at No-man's Land Island, about twenty miles to the west, where it is often necessary to go after them with deep-running lures on wire or weighted lines.

The fish we caught had alewives and squid in their stomachs. The alewives will soon depart, having completed their spawning runs in freshwater streams, but the squid and the blues will be around all summer.

Maine's Saco River Seldom Fails to Produce Good Striper Fishing

Saco, Maine

Within the shadows of the river cities of Saco and Biddeford, we took striped bass on both the rising and the falling tides from midmorning to midafternoon.

And this, said our guide, Robert Boilard of Biddeford, is the rule, rather than the exception.

Boilard is one of two guides on the four-and-a-half-mile stretch of the Saco from the cities to the river's mouth in Saco Bay. A power dam at the upper end of this stretch is the end of the journey for the alewives and stripers that run up the river each spring to spawn. The other guide is sixty-eight-year-old Jim Trickey, who was out alone the day we fished, working the flats with a fly rod and popping plug.

Informed anglers have long been aware of the Saco's striped bass, but there has been no real fishing pressure on the river. The classic and time-honored striper grounds, such as those off Cape Cod, Cuttyhunk, and Martha's Vineyard in Massachusetts, and Narragansett Bay and Chesapeake Bay, have attracted more attention. Of Maine's striper rivers, which have gone virtually untouched, the Saco is probably the best.

A few large bass, thirty pounds or more, are caught in the Saco, but Boilard is quick to say that most of the bass are school fish, five to ten pounds.

What the Saco offers is action. Indeed, Boilard is so sure of the river's productivity that for years he told clients, "No fish, no pay." This somewhat daring guaranty no longer exists, but in the last two years Boilard has had only two days in which his boat took no fish, and on both occasions several bass were hooked but lost.

Victor Pomiecko of Claremont, New Hampshire, and I caught twenty stripers, from three to eight pounds, in five hours of fishing with Boilard. Several of the smaller bass were tagged and released. (The tags, which were supplied by the American Littoral Society of Sandy Hook, New Jersey, provide information on growth and migration if the fish are recaptured.)

All our stripers were taken by trolling eight-inch Burke worms riding in tandem with a hook baited with sandworms.

"I know you gentlemen would rather cast to the fish," Boilard said when we arrived at the Biddeford and Saco Yacht Club, where he keeps his boat, "but it is a little early in the season for that. Later there will be plenty of action on both surface and underwater lures, or even fly rods."

The stripers, which arrived a little after the alewives in the spring, will be around through September, Boilard said.

A few fishermen on shore and from a boat were going for large stripers with chunks of cut alewives, and a thirty-pounder had been taken by that method that very week.

Boilard is initimately acquainted with every hole, eddy, bar, and flat in the river, from the dam to the bay, and many times he announced beforehand where a fish would hit. His clients over the past several years have come from thirty-nine of the fifty states and from Canada.

When the average hunter or fisherman looks at a map of Maine, he thinks of deer and bears or trout, landlocked salmon, and Atlantic salmon. A day with Boilard will persuade him to add striped bass to the list. Many of Maine's rivers, including the Sheepscott and Damariscotta, provide excellent striper angling.

Boilard's address, for those who might like to reserve a day of fishing with him, is 19 High Street, Biddeford, Maine 04005.

Gadabout Gaddis Gives Lesson on Kennebec River Smallmouth Bass

Skowhegan, Maine

Whirling out from under a stump along the banks of the Kennebec River, the smallmouth bass engulfed the popping plug in a shower of spray.

"Wow! Boy, oh, boy! Oh, how I love it when they hit like that!" said R. V. "Gadabout" Gaddis from his seat in the bow of our square-ended canoe.

He played the fish for a few minutes on his fly rod, brought him to the boat, and released him.

We had driven from his lodge in Bingham to a point below Skowhegan, where we launched the canoe in a tangle of pulpwood logs.

"This pulpwood is on the river most of the summer, about 285,000 cords each year," he said. "It used to be only in the spring. It's damn foolishness. People don't want to run a boat on a river full of logs. Also the bark falls off many of them and sinks to the bottom, and you can imagine what that does to insect life. We used to see big mayfly hatches. We don't anymore."

As he talked he continued to cast, and Gaddis knows how to handle a fly rod. For an hour he dropped his popping plug within a few inches of snags, logs, and rocks or skidded it under overhanging branches.

Once in a while he would, of course, get hung up. While untangling one such mess he said, "You know, when I'm filming a show I include things like this. If I made a bad cast I let the people see it. That, I think, is one of the reasons for the show's success. People know I'm no different than they are."

Gaddis was referring to his television show, "Gadabout Gaddis, the Flying Fisherman," which is sponsored by the Liberty Mutual Insurance Company.

"Also, I stay away from plush resorts, places where the average man couldn't go. And I've been on streams where the state fish and game people have offered to stock it with big trout just for the show. I tell them No, that I want to show it as it really is."

In swift succession he caught half a dozen more bass and then said, "Your turn. Put her ashore and we'll change seats."

He watched me catch a few bass and then said, "Mind if I make a suggestion?"

Assured that I wouldn't mind, he said, "I think you'd attract more fish if you didn't pop the plug so hard. Hit it with a lot of slack line."

I tried his suggestion and it worked.

In three hours we caught and released twelve or fifteen bass, then, as dusk dropped over the river, Gaddis said, "I guess we'd better crank her up and head back. Too dangerous with these logs after dark."

He sat in the bow spotting the logs for me, and nothing less than full throttle would satisfy him—a speed I thought improper, but he was, after all, the host.

Bittersweet Odor
of Burning Peat
Greets Traveler in Scotland

Halkirk, Scotland

Creeping through the dark, rambling halls of Lochdhu Lodge, the bittersweet odor of peat burning in the drawing-room fireplace evoked memories.

A quarter of a century ago, the war in Europe over, I had visited Scotland's Highlands; I had not smelled burning peat since. On the first visit I was pursuing a Scottish lassie with hair as black as a raven's wing, but this time the quarry was salmon and trout. Such are the ages of man.

Lochdhu Lodge looms out of a vast, remote moor in northern Scotland's Caithness County. Laird of the manor is Robin Sinclair, a tall, handsome man who flew Spitfires in World War II. (Sinclair's father, Viscount Thurso, Churchill's wartime air minister, died this June. His title passes on to Robin Sinclair.)

Robin Sinclair, or Lord Thurso, controls some sixty thousand acres of grouse and stag moors and the salmon fishing rights on the Thurso River, which rises in the Knockfin Heights and runs forty miles in a northerly direction to the sea. From spring into fall, sportsmen from Britain, the Continent, and the United States journey to Sinclair's holdings in quest of fish and game. Americans usually make bookings through Winchester Adventures, Inc., 100 Park Avenue, New York, New York 10017, although they may, if they wish, write directly to Lochdhu Hotels, Ltd., Ulster Arms Hotel, Halkirk, Caithness, Scotland.

Driving the twenty miles from Halkirk to Lochdhu in a rental car, I soon entered a single-track dirt road. The purple bloom was on the heather and to my left the twin peaks of three-thousand-foot Morven in the Caithness Hills provided a constant navigational reference. (I knew Lochdhu was about ten miles north of Morven.) Sheep grazed on the moors, and one often had to stop for them; hares and rabbits made frequent showings, and I also put up several coveys of grouse.

When one is making the drive at the tag end of a wearying series of air connections from the United States—in my case, the entire trip consumed twenty-two hours—it seems as if Lochdhu is at the end of the world. The road reaches on and on—sometimes in the valley of the Thurso, sometimes skirting dark, peat-stained lochs, past dark piles of cut peat, past tiny hilltop graveyards—until at last one sees the stone tower of Lochdhu, built in 1895 by Sir Tollemache Sinclair as a shooting lodge, lifting abruptly out of the dark, cloud-capped moors.

But at the end of the journey all is well. There is the glowing peat fire in the drawing room, the gracious greeting from Benjamin Brind, the resident manager, and his charming wife, Eve, a tot of malt whisky, and a wide bed warmed by a hot-water bottle.

I had noted on the drive to Lochdhu that the Thurso seemed quite low, and when the river is not in spate the salmon do not choose to swim up it to spawn. Brind confirmed this observation.

"The river is low, and fishing has not been good on the upper beats," he said. "We need three days of good rain to bring the fish up."

But that news was not depressing. One important goal, reaching Lochdhu, had been attained. In that strange twilight the moors and the hills held an unearthly beauty that persists until past midnight this far north at this time of year, and if the salmon would not cooperate there were brown trout to be had in the remote and lovely lochs in the hills about us.

And on a height in the moors across the dark lake that is Lochdhu a stag and his hinds appeared on the skyline; then, as one strained to watch them in the ghostly light, they seemed to fade out of sight, as unsubstantial as a dream.

Grouse Fly
As Shooters Go Forth
on "Glorious Twelfth"
in Scotland

Halkirk, Scotland

Heavy clouds sometimes obscured the sun, but the air was clear as we moved in a long line up the hill over heather, sedge, and sphagnum moss, and far below us the Thurso River gleamed in its green valley.

It was the "Glorious Twelfth," the opening of the hunting season for red grouse in the British Isles, and I was on a family shoot with Lord Thurso (Robin Sinclair) and his family.

The party included Lady Thurso and the three Sinclair children, John, 16 years old, Patrick, 15, Camilla, 13, and a young French guest, Corinne Tutin. The hunting began soon after we left Dalnawillan Lodge, the Sinclairs' country place.

At the leading edge of the line was William Gunn, gamekeeper at Dalnawillan, with an experienced setter going before him. Gunn's brother, Jack, the gillie, stayed well back with two more setters and a Labrador retriever, the retriever for finding downed birds.

The ubiquitous Scottish midge, a tiny fellow with an authoritative bite, troubled us until we reached the windswept summit of the hill. Shortly thereafter an old cock grouse flushed wild at the left end of the line and was downed by one of the two boys. A few minutes later a covey of six grouse flushed wild at the right end of the line, and Lord Thurso, who was shooting a 12-gauge Purdy, failed to touch a feather with either barrel.

The area, or "beat," we were shooting covered about a thousand acres, as do all the grouse beats on Lord Thurso's moors in northern Scotland's Caithness County. In many parts of the British Isles, grouse are driven over hunters waiting at their stations, or "buts," but one hunts with dogs on Robin Sinclair's moors.

In a little more than an hour's hunting, several coveys, totaling perhaps forty birds, had been located by the setter, and three or four brace of grouse, including a nice double by Lord Thurso, were in Jack Gunn's game bag.

The previous evening at nearby Lochdhu Lodge, where bird hunters from France, Italy, and England had gathered in preparation for opening day, Lord Thurso had presided over the drawing of lots for the various beats. Shells, or cartridges as they are called here, had been dispensed, and all the gunners had been in bed by midnight.

Lord Thurso confessed that he did not know when the Glorious Twelfth came into being, but at Lochdhu Lodge there is the diary of a man who hunted the area more than a century ago. The entry for August 11, 1856, has him arriving on the scene, and on August 12 he records shooting 47½ brace of grouse, ninety-five birds, a rather remarkable achievement for the days of muzzle loading. One must assume that the man who loaded for him was covered with black powder residue by the end of the day.

Individual bags are smaller today, but by American upland bird-shooting standards, they are enormous. In the 1969 season, ten guns on Sinclair's moors killed 1,173 brace of grouse, and the best day's bag by a two-man party was thirty-four brace. Each gun is allowed to keep a brace of grouse a day. Most of the shooters on Lord Thurso's moors are repeaters, and bookings are made early in the year.

There are no bag limits on grouse. A good gamekeeper knows how much shooting a moor will stand, and parties are booked accordingly. For example, Lord Thurso's one-thousand-acre beats are shot over about once every three weeks.

The tradition of the Glorious Twelfth also extends to the eating of grouse. Tonight at Lochdhu, grouse shot during the day will be served, and the same is true of certain London hotels. At the posh Savoy, for example, a hotel spokesman said that young grouse shot on the Yorkshire moors this morning were being flown in for the evening's menu.

"We have even got a grouse fly, a fly that one finds in the birds' feathers, to prove this," the same spokesman said after being asked whether frozen birds from last year would be offered.

Those eating Yorkshire grouse at the Savoy this evening will pay seventy-five shillings (nine dollars) a bird. This does not include the vegetables.

Other birds are being flown to hotels in New York and Paris, where they were expected to be on tonight's dinner tables.

With Viscount Handling the Dogs, American Is a Bit Uneasy

Halkirk, Scotland

In one of Dickens' novels a gentleman bird-shooting for the first time in his life has a miserable start, but performs brilliantly after shutting both eyes and firing into the blue.

Once, during my first half-hour on Viscount Thurso's grouse moors in northern Scotland's Caithness County, I thought of emulating Dickens' character, having missed two easy straightway shots, but after scratching out a shaky double, then a clean one, I relaxed and performed in creditable fashion.

There was, at least from my point of view, considerable pressure on me to shoot reasonably well, for Lord Thurso, Robin Sinclair, had worked me into a tight shooting schedule, and when the gamekeeper who was to have taken me afield fell ill, he had announced that he would be my gamekeeper for the day. One does not often have a viscount, who is also an excellent wing shot, for a gamekeeper.

The other shooter, or gun, was thirteen-year-old Patrick Sinclair, Lord Thurso's youngest son. In about an hour and a half of tramping over the heather in the morning, we took five and one half brace (eleven birds), and in a shorter period in the afternoon four and one half brace.

A gusty west wind sweeping across the moors in the morning made the birds extremely nervous, and they frequently flushed wild and nearly out of range of the 20-gauge over and under Winchesters, bored and modified and improved cylinder, that Patrick and I were shooting.

During our lunch break the wind died and hordes of midges rose from the grass and heather and swarmed about our heads, sending us marching back and forth slapping desperately at them. A light breeze will keep midges down, and Lord Thurso was of the opinion that the wind would soon rise again, so we set forth. The wind did rise, but with it came a black cloud full of rain.

We continued to shoot for an hour, until our English setters began to have great difficulty finding birds. Two of the setters were old, but their skill in unraveling the spoor left by grouse moving on the ground over the moor was a pleasure to watch. On several occasions the distance from the first tentative point to the covey covered 150 yards. (All the grouse-shooting on Lord Thurso's moors is with dogs; there are no driven birds.)

Just before the rain began, a herd of red deer appeared over the distant skyline, some thirty or forty stags, hinds, and young animals, looking like a company of advancing infantry. In early fall hunters will be after them.

The rain made me think of the nearby Thurso River. A prolonged dry spell in July and early August had left the river low, and good salmon fishing on it was confined to the lower beats, those near the sea.

David Sinclair, the river superintendent, had told me the day before that great numbers of salmon, more than he had seen in many years, were cruising Thurso Bay at the river's mouth waiting for a spate to begin their upstream procreative journey.

Professor Stewart Shares Knowledge of "Dour" Loch Trout in Scotland

Halkirk, Scotland

Cloud shadows raced over the moors as we climbed slowly to a hilltop loch, Airidh Leathaid, where richly marked brown trout awaited us.

My companion was Dr. Frederick H. Stewart, who heads the department of geology at Edinburgh University. I had tried the remote moor lochs around Lochdhu Hotel in northern Scotland's Caithness County a few times before with small success, but Stewart's presence gave me comfort.

When Joe Fitzpatrick, a gillie at Lochdhu and also a student sculptor, heard that Stewart was taking me under his wing for a try at the loch trout, he was most optimistic.

"The professor is a very keen trout fisherman. He works very hard at it, and I wish I knew what he knows about loch fishing," he said.

The large trout in the lochs about Lochdhu Hotel are either remarkably sophisticated or remarkably recalcitrant. Fly-fishing is relatively easy in the lochs, or lakes, that hold only small trout, but when one goes after fish of a pound or more one soon finds that they are, to use a local phrase, very "dour."

Last year the trout from Airidh Leathaid averaged nearly a

pound and a half each. Guests at Lochdhu Hotel may fish all these moor lakes free of charge, and only one man, or one party of anglers, is allowed on any lake each day.

In the United States it is generally accepted that the brook trout is the easiest to capture, the rainbow next in line, and the brown, particularly the larger fish, the most difficult. Some Scottish anglers take large browns with a fly baited with a maggot.

In a hotel lobby in Wick, Scotland, I met George Lockhart, a Glasgow trout angler, who after a moment's conversation kindly presented me with a plastic box crawling with maggots.

"Put one of these on your fly and fish at night," he said. I never used them.

When we reached Airidh Leathaid the professor said, "Tie a Grouse and Claret on the tail of your cast [leader] and use a rather large and bushy fly on your dropper."

I had no Grouse and Claret, so he gave me one of his. Ten casts later a pound-and-a-quarter fish swallowed the Grouse and Claret and twice she danced over the dark, wind-driven waves of the lake. The fish was a female, heavy with roe and apparently about to spawn, for her vent was protruding.

Triumphantly I held my fish over my head so the professor could see it, but he, choosing to drift-fish from a boat, was busy landing a trout of his own, slightly smaller than mine.

Reverently placing my not-so-dour trout in a bower of heather, I returned to the attack full of hope.

"It was the Grouse and Claret all along," I thought. "With the Grouse and Claret I am master of these fish."

Four hours and two hundred casts later I was humble once again. I had danced my Grouse and Claret and its companion along the water. I had fished them slow and deep and fast and deep —I had twice managed to land them on rising fish, and rising fish were rare, all to no avail.

The professor, meanwhile, drifted and cast, rowed back and drifted and cast, again and again. A keen fisherman indeed, but he, veteran angler of the lochs, had no more success than I.

At the end of the day as we shared a cup of coffee on the shore of the lake, the professor told me that he had first fished these lakes on a visit to the area with his wife, the novelist Mary Stewart.

"One never really knows when the fish will take," he said. "I've never been able to observe any real pattern."

As we hiked back to the road the sharp west wind died, then rose again, bringing a brief shower of rain; the dark hills were half shrouded in mist, and a gray cloud covered the summit of three-thousand-foot Morven, the giant of the Caithness Plain.

There were other days of loch and salmon fishing with my new friend, and at the end of those few days it seemed as if I had known that charming and witty man all my life.

Our last evening was spent on Glut Loch, and as a nearly full moon hung between the dark twin peaks of Morven and red grouse cackled on the moors about us, Professor Stewart caught one trout of a pound and a half and we were content.

Curlews Cry through a Night on the Naver, But Trout Elusive

Bettyhill, Scotland

Unseen overhead, curlews cried in the soft night as the incoming tide moved up the mouth of the River Naver in northern Scotland.

"You needn't wade out very far," said my companion and gillie for the evening, Walter Carruthers of Thurso, "and you may hear them splashing, ken, out there before you, ken?"

The "they" that might be heard splashing before me were sea trout, and it was sea trout that we were after.

"And if one takes," said Walter, "he may go straightaway into the air. Do you ken?"

I kenned indeed and began to cast, throwing my line with its small dark fly, a Stoat's Tail, across the broad estuary toward a black hillside.

Walter and I had arrived at the mouth of the Naver shortly after 10 P.M. We had dawdled in his cottage in Thurso, drinking tea and coffee and munching through mounds of sandwiches and cake prepared by his wife, Margaret, a Belfast girl whose classic blond beauty will stop a man dead in his tracks.

"Walter," I had asked, "with so lovely a wife how can you bring yourself to be fishing so many of your evenings away?"

"Ah, Nelson, it's my job, do you ken? And she understands. Do you not understand, darlin'?"

Her soft smile held both amusement and understanding.

Not long ago Walter held a regular job at the nearby Dounreay atomic energy research plant, but punching a time clock was not for him. His love was for the moors and game birds and shooting, and fishing for salmon and trout.

An hour's casting in the estuary brought no fish, and we moved above the bridge to a pool where Walter had obtained permission from the water bailiff to fish for sea trout. The Naver is a good salmon river, a private salmon river, and during the daylight the pool we fished would be off limits, but at night, when sea trout are caught, salmon do not often hit.

By 3 A.M. Walter was in despair. The wind, which had been providing a much-needed ripple, had died, and in the growing light from the east the pool gleamed smooth. Once a sea trout jumped in front of me but would not take, and several times salmon burst from the water, showering me with spray.

"We will do nothing without a breeze," said Walter, who had raised, but failed to hook, one sea trout. (The sea trout quite possibly may be a brown trout turned anadromous, although there seemed to be no agreement on this among the local anglers I consulted.)

With the loss of the breeze, the midges rose from the grass and attacked. The demonic Scottish midge's bite compares favorably with that of the black fly of the forests of northern New England, and unlike the black fly, he does not go to bed with the sun.

With the first substantial light of dawn, about four o'clock, the salmon began to move upriver. We could see their broad backs as they splashed through the shallows at the upper end of the pool.

By that time the patrol against poaching by netters, maintained by the water bailiff and his helpers, had ended, and in the strange half-light we saw two dark figures in the distance scurrying toward the river. They were, Walter thought, another form of poacher: worm fishermen who could not resist the impulse to try for a salmon or two before the world awakened.

Lawyer, Wife, and Sons Practice Art of Falconry on Remote Moors

Halkirk, Scotland

Hovering above the dark moor and above the pointing setter, the two peregrine falcons waited for another dog, a spaniel, to flush the covey of grouse.

Even from one hundred yards distant, the leather jesses (straps) on the birds' legs could be seen, and the tinkling of the tiny bells they also wore was borne down the wind.

When the grouse (there were three of them) went up, both falcons went after the first to become airborne, dropping in a short stoop, or dive, using the speed of the stoop to overtake their quarry. One of the falcons hit the grouse, there was a puff of feathers, and the stricken bird tumbled into the heather. A falcon strikes with its three front claws doubled up, like a fist. The outstretched back claw, with its sharp talon, knifes into the prey.

The successful falcon was allowed, as a reward, to eat the head and neck of the grouse it had killed, before the falconer, Geoffrey Pollard, picked it up and replaced its hood. The other falcon sat nearby on a hummock, waiting for the hunt to resume.

"That was not particularly good," said Pollard, apparently referring to the failure of the second falcon to make a kill. He noted that his birds were in various stages of molt and therefore lacked considerable speed and maneuverability. Also, he said, they often hover at a great height, making long, spectacular stoops on their prey.

Falconry, which dates back to before the time of Christ, is still practiced by a few men in various corners of the world, and Pollard, a lawyer who lives at Endlands, Heronsgate-near-Rickmansworth, Hertfordshire, England, is one of the best, particularly at hawking red grouse, according to Lord Thurso, Robin Sinclair, on whose moors Pollard was hunting.

Pollard favors the peregrine, or female, falcon (the smaller male is often called a tercel) because, as he puts it, "she is larger and deadlier."

When hawking on Lord Thurso's moors, Pollard keeps his birds in a stone outbuilding adjoining Dalnawillan Lodge, the lord's summer place, and one steps back through centuries when entering that shadowy mews. In the half-light of the place, the magnificent, hooded birds sit on a long rail that traverses the interior. Some have red hoods, some tan; their yellow talons grip the rail firmly, and there is a faint tinkling of bells when the birds move.

On the floor is the rectangular wooden frame, or cadge, on which the hooded birds are carried afield, and on the wall the leather gauntlets that falconers wear when handling the birds, and the fabric-covered horseshoe, or lure, with line and bait attached, which the falconer whirls about his head to bring his birds to him.

Falconry calls for total dedication, and the lean, intense Pollard appears to have no lack in this regard. His hawking is a family affair. His ten-year-old son, James, carries the cadge, his twelve-year-old son, Nicholas, handles the spaniel that flushes the grouse, and his trim and lovely wife, Diana, may have one of two setters and three more spaniels on leashes, or a nervous falcon that does not like the cadge riding on her wrist.

Mrs. Pollard understands and shares her husband's fascination for falconry. Remarkably fit, she can easily spring one hundred yards across the rough moorland with three leashed dogs lunging on before.

The falcons do, of course, have a profound effect on the Pollards' lives. After experimenting with leaving the birds in another's care, Pollard decided it was not wise, and one cannot stay at a typical hotel or vacation resort with a room full of falcons that must be fed and put out to "weather" each day so they may preen themselves.

"We lead, therefore," says Mrs. Pollard, "very quiet lives."

Pollard, now in his early forties, began hawking as a teen-ager, but he may be, in his own words, "at the zenith" of his hawking career. The laws of the various countries where falcons may be found are making it difficult to purchase them, and when they can be bought they are becoming more and more expensive. An untrained bird may cost two hundred dollars. Pollard's birds come from such widely separated spots as North Carolina, the Persian Gulf, and Scotland. His most experienced peregrine, Aurora, is from America and is ten years old. She may live to twice that age.

What is the relationship between falconer and falcon? Mrs. Pollard was asked.

When it was possible to have a young bird (an eyass) from the nest, she said, they often showed affection for the falconer, regarding him as a parent figure. Wild-trapped tercels can be affectionate, she added, but never the female falcon.

"I believe the peregrines only tolerate us—tolerate us because we provide them with the hunting they want," she said.

Her husband noted that while a falcon captured as an eyass often showed affection, its hunting instinct was muted because it had never learned to fend for itself.

Lord Thurso's rolling grouse moors are superb for hawking, the Pollards say, and other falconers, some from the Continent, often pursue their passion there.

Several evenings after hawking with the Pollards, I joined them for dinner in the small stone cottage they rent, hard by the tiny, moor-surrounded Altnabreac railway station, which no longer has a stationmaster.

Our fare was perhaps the rarest dish in the world, red grouse killed by a falcon. The birds were young and tender, and one did not, Pollard noted, have to worry about shotgun pellets.

More than two thousand years before, falconers and their families dined similarly, for hawks, the goshawk in particular, were tools with which to gather food.

Uncleaned Fish Impossible Hurdle for Most American Housewives

Some housewives are reluctant to cook the fish their husbands bring home. Part of this reluctance may be attributed to an olfactory fastidiousness—many women don't like the odor left behind in the kitchen after the fish is done. However, the husband is often responsible for his wife's negative attitude toward the bounty he gathers from the sea.

A man should not stagger into the house with a bushel of glassy-eyed bluefish, sling them into the kitchen sink, and cry happily, "Here's supper, honey."

There are some stalwart ladies, daughters of lobster men, nieces of sea captains, who will dive into a school of dead fish with a keen knife and squeals of delight, but they are rare.

What usually happens is that the husband—after allowing his children to poke at the fish with nervous fingers and hearing them ask, always, "Are they dead?"—turns the kitchen into an abattoir, and when he has finished there is slime in the sink, scales on the walls, and blood in his wife's eye.

The first rule of the game is to clean the fish outdoors. One can set up an old table for this, at a suitable distance from the house, and a water hose should be nearby.

Cleaning fish is an easily learned skill. Let us consider four species common off the East Coast of the United States: striped bass, bluefish, Atlantic mackerel, and summer flounder, or fluke. Of these, the striper has the largest scales, the blues and flounders follow, and the mackerel needs no scaling.

It is good, whenever possible, to scale fish soon after they are caught. Scales adhere tenaciously after the fish dries out.

A simple and fast way to clean blues, mackerel, and stripers is to take a single fillet from each side. A sharp, slender knife should be used, and the blade should be at least eight inches long for fish over five pounds. With such a tool a man can start at the tail of the fish and make one pass along the backbone to the head, repeating the process on the other side. This takes only a few seconds, and 95 per cent of the meat is removed.

The traditional way to clean a flounder is to take two fillets from each side after a cut has been made down to the bone along the lateral lines of the fish. If the blue or bass is small, say three to five pounds, he may be baked whole. In that case, he would be scaled and gutted and the head left on.

If the fisherman presents his wife with fresh fillets carefully wrapped in aluminum foil, he will find her happy to cooperate in the cooking.

One further bit of advice to anglers: it is not good form to present one's friends with uncleaned fish. Such fish usually wind up in the garbage pail, and the friend and his wife must, on a subsequent day, tell a lie.

Shakespeare Comes in with the Fog on Remote Cuttyhunk Island

Cuttyhunk Island, Massachusetts

In twilight at land's end at Cuttyhunk, fog, driven by a strong southerly wind, rolled in from the ocean and swept past in jagged streams, and above the sustained moaning of the surf and the grinding of rocks on the shore, I thought I heard Shakespeare's Caliban speaking:

> I prithee let me bring thee where crabs grow;
> And I with my long nails will dig thee pig-nuts;
> Show thee a jay's nest and instruct thee how
> To snare the nimble marmoset. . . .

I had been set on my imaginative course by Mrs. Louise T. Haskell, former teacher at Cuttyhunk's one-room schoolhouse and currently the island's librarian. It was she who brought to my attention that in 1902 Dr. Edward Hale had advanced the theory that Cuttyhunk quite possibly was the setting for Shakespeare's *Tempest*.

To the north, through a momentary opening in the fog, I glimpsed a lush, almost tropical valley, a tangle of vines, briars, bayberry bushes, and other shrubs, and a stone tower on an islet in West End Pond, the monument to the English explorer and navigator Bartholomew Gosnold, who landed on Cuttyhunk in 1602, and built, where the tower now stands, "the first English habitation on the coast of New England."

Hale's evidence for his thesis included the statement that Gosnold's expedition was backed by the Earl of Southampton, Shakespeare's patron.

Site of *The Tempest* or not, Cuttyhunk, the outermost of the Elizabeth Islands, is a remarkable place, perhaps best known among the angling fraternity for its excellent striped bass fishing.

Since World War II, fast, able craft have taken the emphasis off shore fishing at Cuttyhunk, but I had hoped to fish some of the old stand sites on the Vineyard Sound side of the island. Four days of strong winds and the resulting heavy surf made this impossible.

On the fourth day Charles Spanos of Claremont, New Hampshire, and I borrowed an outboard runabout belonging to our host and Cuttyhunk summer resident, Millard Ashley of Attleboro, Massachusetts, and ran along the Buzzard's Bay side of the island of Nashawena to Quicks Hole, the passage between Nashawena and Pasque Island.

Several other boats were working the area but we saw no fish caught, and by late afternoon the fog once again closed in over the island.

By seven that evening we could see only a portion of the harbor from our vantage point of Ashley's verandah a quarter of a mile away, and overhead, for more than thirty minutes, we could hear and sometimes glimpse the Cessna float plane piloted by Norman Gingras of Rochester, Massachusetts, trying to find a hole in the fog so he could land.

Gingras, who operates a charter service to the Elizabeths, Martha's Vineyard, and Nantucket, finally gave up and returned home.

Wahoo Caught
Off Hatteras Inlet Provides
Tasty Meal That Evening

Hatteras, North Carolina

Music—it was something of Brahms's—came fitfully down the wind to us as we rolled in three-foot seas offshore from Hatteras Inlet.

The music, which came from Diamond Shoals light, a Texas tower manned by Coast Guard personnel off North Carolina's Outer Banks, blended with the excited cries of terns diving after bait fish and the sound of the sea surging against the giant steel legs of the tower, which are anchored in the ocean bottom more than fifty feet below.

"The last time we were here we picked up several nice king mackerel by casting Hopkins lures to the base of the tower," said our skipper, Bob Smirnow.

But even though Smirnow's twenty-three-foot launch *Yellowbird* has a deep, ocean-racing hull, the rough water made casting difficult and we compromised by trolling. Almost immediately something hit one of our lures, a red-feathered jig, and when I had reeled the fish close enough to see a shimmering in the clear green water, three large, dark shapes rose in pursuit. One of them struck the hooked fish, an eight-pound king mackerel, severing it in a ragged line just behind the head.

The larger fish, which we were unable to identify, left as quickly as they had appeared, and we saw no more of them.

An hour later, more than a mile from the tower, Joel Arrington, outdoor editor of the travel and promotion division of the North Carolina Department of Conservation and Development, hooked a six-pound dolphin. Several of its mates escorted it to the boat, and we cast to them with fly rods and big streamers, which they followed but did not hit.

Leaving the vicinity of the tower, Smirnow ran the *Yellowbird* ten or fifteen miles more offshore to the blue water of the Gulf Stream. Powered by two 130-horsepower outdrive engines, the *Yellowbird* can approach thirty knots. This probably seems slow to her skipper, who is a jet pilot for United Air Lines. In addition to his flying, Smirnow owns the Hatteras Marine and Trading Company.

We had hoped to catch white marlins and sailfish in the Gulf Stream, and although we failed in this, we did boat one splendid prize, a thirty-three-pound wahoo that hit Arrington's lure. The wahoo, a long, lean, powerful fish and one of the fastest in the ocean, gave Arrington a good tussle for ten minutes before yielding. He was taken on fifty-pound-test line.

Smirnow trolls the Gulf Stream with rather light gear: the fifty-pound rig is usually the heaviest he uses.

We had wahoo steaks for supper and found them good, similar to swordfish in taste and texture.

Marlin fishing, for both whites and blues, has been excellent this year off the Outer Banks. By mid-August more than five hundred whites and fifty-nine blues had been brought in by boats working out of the Fishing Center at Oregon Inlet. On one day alone this summer, sixty-two whites came into the Fishing Center. The blues have ranged from one "baby" of thirty-nine pounds, a most unusual catch, to a giant 626-pounder taken by Ronald Craft of Plymouth, North Carolina.

Rapids on Maine's Allagash River Too Much for Some Canoeists

Churchill Lake, Maine

Girls in bikinis and young men in bathing trunks were negotiating Chase Rapids on the Allagash River with varying degrees of success when we launched our two canoes in the pool below Churchill Lake Dam.

Some of the canoes, and the majority were aluminum craft built by Grumman, got through without mishap. Others missed the channel, and their occupants had to get out and push; still others hit rocks at full speed, swung sideways, and filled with water, toppling their occupants into the rushing river. There was little danger involved, however, for the water was warm and for the most part shallow.

Ben Pike, regional public relations representative for the International Paper Company, was stern man in my craft, wielding a steel-shod canoe pole with what appeared to be commendable dexterity.

Pole man in the other canoe of our four-man party was Camille Beaulieu of Lac Frontière, Maine. Beaulieu is an experienced guide, riverman, and trapper, and also drives the mail run from Daaquan, Quebec, to Clayton Lake, Maine, along the IP logging road. Riding with Beaulieu was Victor Pomiecko of Claremont, New Hampshire.

Beaulieu's mastery of canoe poling was evident immediately. Standing in the stern of his twenty-foot Grumman, the short, muscular man made his craft dart along the river like a water strider. Moving the canoe to the right or left, or upstream or downstream, with seemingly effortless ease, he studied each nasty bit of water carefully before dropping through.

Not content with poling his own canoe, he shouted directions to all other craft above and below him, cautioning, praising, cajoling incessantly. Despite his efforts, six or seven canoes went aground or hit rocks and filled with water, and flotation cushions, paddles, duffel bags, and sundry other bits of gear were soon floating downstream.

Because there was no danger, the scene amused me, and a moment later I was able to laugh at myself; Pike's pole slipped on the bottom, the bow of our canoe lodged against a rock, the stern swung round and jammed against another rock, and in a twinkling we were overboard and the canoe was broadside to the current.

Pike and I were unable to move the craft, a lovely wood and canvas Old Towner, so I busied myself with taking pictures of our dilemma, bracing my legs against a huge boulder in the rushing, waist-deep water. (I was using a waterproof Nikonos camera and seemed assured of several good pictures, including some of other more successful river runners racing by, but later discovered that I had failed to load the camera properly.)

With the help of Beaulieu, Pomiecko, and two husky scouts from Explorer Post 33 of Derby, Connecticut, who were also running the Allagash, we dislodged our craft and floated her battered, water-filled hulk into the shallows. Both gunwales were broken, as well as twelve ribs, three planks, one seat, and one thwart; but she had no holes in her, and we gathered up our gear, which was in waterproof bags, climbed aboard, and followed Beaulieu and Pomiecko through the last bad stretch of Chase Rapids. We stopped for lunch and then continued to the lower end of Umsasksis Lake, where we made camp at the so-called Ledges on the east shore, one of the authorized campsites on the Allagash Waterway.

Supper, cooked in the open over a stone fireplace, included several excellent steaks, boiled potatoes, peas, canned peaches, and a tot of bourbon for all hands.

A few hours after sunset we crawled into our sleeping bags. Overhead in the tall conifers, a gentle southerly breeze (a breeze that would bring rain, Beaulieu said) whispered softly; small waves lapped against the rocks on the shore, and somewhere on the darkened lake a loon wailed.

Fall

A Partridge in the Bush
As Good As One in the Hand

Newport, New Hampshire

One of the charming things about partridge hunting is that you don't have to kill a bird to be pleased.

Just putting a few up will make the day satisfactory. It is something like glimpsing a beautiful woman in a crowd. You'll never touch her or know her, but you are happier for the fleeting vision.

Fleeting visions were all I got of partridges here in a two-hour tour through mixed hardwoods and hemlocks off the Chapin Pond Road.

Fall's tattered ensigns littered the forest floor, most of them flung there by the previous evening's heavy rain.

It was a good day for hunting partridges. Most of the leaves were off the trees, giving more visibility, and there was no wind—an important thing also. The birds are almost always heard before they are seen, and the wind fills the woods with noise.

I went in a half mile to a hillside covered with big beeches and an occasional hemlock. Partridges like beechnuts, and so do I. I looked for the tasty triangular nuts, but found only empty hulls—the squirrels and partridges had been there ahead of me. I did find the tracks of two deer, one large and one small, made earlier in the day.

A red squirrel slid around the side of an adjoining tree and barked derision. Tail arched and quivering, body pumping like a bellows, he yelped at me until, getting no response, he popped back into a hole in his hemlock home. Ten minutes later a gray squirrel rattled through the leaves twenty feet away. I escaped his notice. Chickadees came and went, a jay screamed, and the woods were silent.

I arose, took two steps, and stopped, my feet in shooting position. It is important when hunting partridges always to stop in a shooting stance, for the birds frequently choose that moment to jump.

I wasn't prepared, however, for the huge hemlock that stood between me and the birds when they jumped. There was a throb of wings, a few shaking branches, and just a fleeting vision.

Through the crowd of trees, I saw the general direction taken by one proud head and followed, through a dark glen, across a little swamp and into a dense stand of balsam. One bird flushed again, from almost over my head, but there was no room to bring up the gun. I listened, heard the battering wings stop, and heard the bird land on the ground and run a little way. Pushing through the balsam, I came to a clearing on the hillside and sat for fifteen minutes. At the end of that time I rose and made a mistake. As one should be in shooting stance when stopping, one should also be in shooting stance when starting.

The partridge jumped only thirty feet to my left. I had no time to shift my feet and mount my weapon. This time the flight was long and I did not follow.

Once while leaving the darkening woods I heard a slight scrabbling sound far overhead. High in a huge oak an old porcupine sat. I pondered shooting him. They are bountied (fifty cents) in New Hampshire because of the damage they do to trees. But as I looked at him I saw the trees that had simply grown old and died, trees broken by storms, trees stunted by others that for years had stolen their sunlight, and the bristly silent old fellow high above didn't seem to deserve destruction. He was no vision but he was one of the crowd and somehow important.

New York State Woodcock Plentiful, But Foliage Is Too Heavy

Greene, New York

All about us in the young aspens, birch, and hawthorne, woodcock towered skyward or fluttered above the ground in short flights before dipping down again.

Sometimes they ran along the ground without flushing, forcing Bill Bartlett's twelve-year-old English setter, Chief, to work out their spoor in the sodden leaves.

The fluttering, walking woodcock would have troubled a less experienced dog, but Chief refused to be hurried and moved with great calm and dignity, neither too fast nor too slow and never breaking point to flush a bird.

Bartlett and Bob Maxon, both of Greene, John Falk, public relations manager for Winchester-Western, and I found an excellent woodcock covert late in the afternoon of the first day of our combined woodcock and grouse hunt in the country surrounding Greene, a small community in western New York State.

We located a few woodcock in the morning and bagged four by noon. Nearly a dozen ruffed grouse were flushed, but the heavy foliage gave us no chance to shoot. There had been only one light frost in the area this fall, Bartlett said, and most of the leaves were still aloft.

Within minutes after we entered the woodcock covert, birds were on the wing. Many were seen only fleetingly before they disappeared behind the green canopy of the thick shrubbery, but occasionally a bird broke into the open, affording a shot. Perhaps two dozen shells were needed to bag eight of these birds, a decent performance for such heavy cover. Fish and game department statistics in Pennsylvania, for example, indicate that hunters bag 40 per cent of the woodcock they flush. This figure includes birds shot at more than once, it being relatively simple to mark the flight of a woodcock for a second or even a third attempt.

Although no really accurate tally was possible, we estimated that we had flushed three dozen birds in an hour, and as we worked our way out of the undergrowth to the woods road, where our car was parked, we were content, for it had been a classic woodcock shoot. Content also was the aging Chief, who, on his first hunt of the year, was bone-weary.

Falk and I had planned to try the food at Baron's Restaurant that evening, but the lean, ebullient Bartlett and his charming wife, Billie, would have none of that, and we dined with them and Maxon and his wife, Shirley, at the Bartlett home, where the women bore the spate of masculine talk of great deeds afield with great good humor, an absolute requirement for those who would marry upland bird hunters.

New Brunswick Bans Shooting for Woodcock; DDT the Cause

When the Canadian government announced last month that there would be no hunting season for woodcock in New Brunswick province this fall, it was, to this writer's knowledge, the first time in North America that a game bird had been ruled off-limits because concentrations of DDT it contained were considered a menace to public health.

Canada has already had experience with closing a hunting season because of a dangerous substance found in birds: last fall in the province of Alberta the pheasant season was shut down because of mercury contamination.

The woodcock, whose favorite diet is earthworms, ranges from southeast Manitoba to southern Quebec and Newfoundland, and south through roughly the eastern half of the United States to Louisiana and Florida. It is migratory in the northern portions of its range.

This year the Canadian Wildlife Service and the Food and Drug Directorate of the Canadian Department of Health and Welfare closed the woodcock season when an average of more than 60 parts per million (ppm) were found in the fatty tissues of adult and immature birds shot by researchers early in September in New Brunswick. The Canadian government considers 7 ppm the maximum allowable for human consumption.

DDT concentrations in the New Brunswick birds this year ranged from 3 to 773 ppm. (The birds were tested for DDT this year because similar tests last year revealed concentrations approaching near-dangerous levels.)

Research has established that DDT is a cancer-causing agent in rats and mice. Until recently DDT had been used extensively in the forests of New Brunswick to control the spruce budworm. According to Tony Keith, who heads the pesticide section of the Canadian Wildlife Service, the amount of DDT found in the New Brunswick woodcock varies directly with the intensity of DDT spraying in the various areas where the birds were shot, although eight birds from an area where there had been no spraying averaged 6 ppm.

Recently the Canadian government severely restricted the use of DDT and announced its intent to ban it entirely when suitable substitutes are found.

There is no evidence, according to Keith and Brian C. Carter, director of Fish and Wildlife for the New Brunswick Department of Natural Resources, that the DDT now in New Brunswick woodcock has done any damage to the birds themselves, although this possibility is under investigation.

Keith said that some hunters had argued that even though DDT in the woodcock is above accepted tolerance levels, there would be little danger in the average sportsman's eating the few birds he shot each year. This same argument, said Keith, has been put forth by those who protest the closing of certain waters to fishing because of mercury contamination in the fish.

"It is my belief," said Keith, "that we should consider those communities where fish or wild game, or both, are an important part of the everyday diet." It is wrong, he continued, to consider dropping restrictions because most people would probably not be adversely affected.

At least one of the New England states is currently engaged in measuring DDT concentrations in woodcock. The migratory nature of the bird may make it difficult to ascertain the source of any contamination that is found.

(This column was published in October, 1970.)

Even in Death the Giant Tuna Retains an Awesome Dignity

Galilee, Rhode Island

It was nearly dawn at Galilee. The moon, low in the western sky, shone on the 138 boats of the tuna sport-fishing fleet and gleamed on the smooth water. Stark against the moon were the flying bridges, rigging, and towers of the boats, and stark also was the huge scaffolding where the tuna hang at the end of each day, and on the ground underneath there were dark stains where the great fish had bled.

All was quiet at 5:30 A.M. Five hours before, the waterfront and finger piers had been alive with the activity that is always part of the United States Atlantic Tuna Tournament, and this, the twenty-sixth annual, was no exception.

The previous evening had been a night for cocktails in a giant circus tent hard by the piers. There the contestants, skippers, mates, guests, and tournament officials had gathered to exchange tuna lore and to speculate on what the third and final day would bring.

Later, when the tent closed, celebrations continued aboard the boats or in town, and the hush of the night was broken by the arrival and departure of private cars and taxis and by the sound of singing and laughter and talk from the moored craft. Occasionally a boat engine would rumble alive as some skipper who hadn't had enough of the water during the day took his guests for a moonlight cruise.

At the close of each day's fishing, the tuna are lifted with a crane from the boats and carried, swinging on a chain, to the scaffold where Ed Fisher, weighmaster, notes their poundage. The weight of each fish is marked on it with paint before it is hung by the tail from the heavy horizontal timber.

Hundreds of people line the rock jetties each evening as the tuna fleet comes in, and hundreds more press against the fence that separates the scaffolding from the public. After the fish are suspended the crowd moves in. Little children are hoisted on their fathers' shoulders, and larger children strain to touch and sometimes stroke the head and flanks of the giant fish. Always the touch is reverential.

These fish somehow seem to be more than fish. Even in death they have dignity. Gradually, as darkness closes in, the crowd disperses and the powerful, leathery, gun-metal-blue bodies of the fish hang harsh in the dying light.

When all the pictures have been taken, and all those who desire intimate contact with the conquered giants of the sea have been satisfied, the yellow crane moves in and the tuna are carried away.

These giant tuna, which may live to fifteen years, are oceanic travelers, although researchers, through recovery of tagged fish, still have only a sketchy idea of their migration patterns. It is generally believed that some of the big tuna that pass the Bahamas in May and June show up off New England and Nova Scotia in summer, and giant tuna tagged off the Bahamas have been captured off Norway.

This year the tuna were sold and the proceeds will be sent to the Woods Hole (Massachusetts) Oceanographic Institution to be used in its tuna research program.

It was most fitting that Frank Mather III, the W.H.O.I. scientist who has guided the tuna and billfish tagging research for years, was aboard one of the seven tournament boats that took fish, Ralph

Stuart's *Oyster Stu,* skippered by Al Reynolds. Stuart set what is probably a tournament record by boating his 473-pound fish in ten minutes. The fish was, incidentally, hooked in the mouth, not deep in the stomach. The latter condition sometimes speeds a tuna's capitulation.

Some Fishermen Won't Cooperate with Mather's Tuna Tagging Program

Woods Hole, Massachusetts

Frank J. Mather III, a scientist at the Woods Hole Oceanographic Institution and one of the country's pioneers in the tagging of oceanic fishes to determine growth rate, migration patterns, and population, has hit a snag in his continuing research with bluefin tuna.

(Relatively small fish, such as bluefish or striped bass, are caught with hook and line or net and taken aboard while a plastic tag is fastened to them. Larger species, such as tuna, are tagged in the water with a small metal dart with plastic streamer attached.)

Many sport fishermen in the New York City area apparently believe, says Mather, that if they cooperate with him by tagging bluefins, or by returning tags from recaptured fish, they will lead commercial seiners to the spot.

Describing the fall, 1968, sport-fishing for small, or school, bluefin (six to seventy pounds) off New York harbor's "17 fathom" grounds as excellent, Mather says, "We have been informed by several reliable sources that many boat captains and other fishermen in the area are not sending in the tags they recover. This is reportedly because they believe the tagging, in some mysterious and unexplained manner, leads the seiners to the area . . . these same sport fishermen advertise the good fishing in the area, both in the press and on their radio telephones.

"It seems difficult for them to understand that without such returns it would be impossible to determine which fisheries are affecting the stocks on which they (the sport fishermen) depend. This has forced us to tag small bluefin from commercial catches, paying a high price for each fish."

Mather is concerned over the diminishing ranks of small bluefins that appear off New England, New York, and New Jersey in summer and fall. In 1968, commercial seining, which yielded about 670 tons of these fish, lasted from July 2 to August 22, in an area between southern New Jersey and southeastern Massachusetts.

Working with the seiners, scientists tagged 219 small bluefins; 38 per cent of these were recaptured almost immediately, most of them by the seiners.

The inescapable conclusion is that the numbers of this age group are diminishing. Indeed, the 1968 commercial landings were only a fraction of the harvest five years before.

Mather notes than an international tuna research panel, working under United Nations auspices, has, in a preliminary report, said that "the group of small bluefin fished off New England is certainly small and heavily exploited."

The work of Mather and others has established that certain pelagic fishes, including bluefin tuna and white marlins, make transoceanic crossings, and there is a growing belief on the part of many experts that some of these species will survive and flourish only if all the nations who fish for them cooperate in landing statistics, research, and, if necessary, protective measures, such as tonnage quotas.

Some fish take a long time to reach optimum growth. A bluefin tuna weighing five hundred pounds is from thirteen to fifteen years old. It is obvious that heavy fishing of this age group would quickly reduce their numbers.

(This column was published in March, 1969.)

139

Father's Letter to a Son Hunting with New Companions

When you were fourteen months old, visiting your grandparents for Christmas, you rode in a pack basket on my back, and the girls in South Station smiled at you.

You were two when I took you to a salt marsh and we sat all day in a flimsy duck blind beneath heavy December clouds watching whitecaps in the cove and tall brown grass bending under the seething rain. At dusk the night herons lurched from their roosts, where Mill Brook drains the foot of the swamp, and you shivered with pleasure at their lugubrious cries and lumbering flight. We walked home in the howling dark through the white oak woods and the wet meadows, you on my shoulders.

You were ten the fall we climbed Sunapee Mountain, and when we reached the top we heard geese calling and they tumbled over the ledges above us, half hidden in the swirling snow, lost in the storm. That night a snowshoe rabbit ran into our tent (we saw his tracks in the morning), and a porcupine tried to steal your boots. Dawn was crackling cold, and you learned that the bark of a white birch, even when wet, will always start a fire.

You were twelve when we went partridge hunting. We rested at noon in the wan sun under an old apple tree on a farm abandoned fifty years before and you found that frozen apples are good.

You were sixteen when we went for rainbow trout on the upper Connecticut River, and the final morning in camp you ate six eggs, a pound of bacon, and twenty-two pancakes.

You were seventeen when you and Vic and I snowshoed into Butternut Pond, towing our toboggan behind. We chopped holes in the ice and caught fat yellow perch and cooked a stew in an iron pot by the rock on the eastern shore.

And now you are twenty-one, in uniform in Vietnam, far from home in a tortured, lovely land whose people are divided.

I can offer little except to tell you that I know how it is to live with death grinning down from a cloud, and I still recall my comrades: a cavalcade of christs sweating the green lumber of their burdens up a thousand unknown hills.

There is, my son, a lovely trout stream in a long and deep ravine in the Carolina mountains I'd like you to see. We'll fish it before the new year is done.

Wild Weather Finds Bluefish Feeding on Long Island Sound

The dawn, no frightened girl "on silver-sandaled feet" but a harridan in sea boots, strode across Long Island Sound, a strong west wind whipping her skirts.

Al Reinfelder and I had launched our twelve-foot aluminum boat a few hours before near Roanoke Point on the Long Island side of the Sound and had trolled along the wild and moon-washed shore for striped bass.

At launching time there was very little wind, and the widely spaced swells were only three feet high. We trolled past high bluffs that shone white in the moonlight and past huge boulders, some of them rearing out of the water two hundred yards from shore and others barely awash, rising streaming and weed-clad from the trough of the swells.

We trolled with a variety of lures, including the plastic eels made by Alou Tackle Company, Inc., of Bayside, Queens. This was only proper, for Reinfelder and a fishing friend, Lou Palma, had founded the company a few years ago. Today the Alou eel, made in various sizes and colors, is one of the East Coast's most productive striper baits. But the bass refused all offerings.

At dawn we stopped trolling and worked likely-looking spots

142

more intensely, casting plugs, jigs, and eels toward the shore. Again there was no action, and our thoughts turned to bluefish. Patroling the ever-roughening water from Roanoke Point west to the little community of Baiting Hollow, we looked for terns.

At first small bands of them flew swiftly over the waves, occasionally dipping down for menhaden, but there seemed to be no concentration of fish under them. Then, at about eight o'clock, more than a hundred birds bunched up, screaming and diving; under them we could see bluefish slashing in a welter of flying spray.

After several minutes of pounding head-on into the seas, we got a hundred yards upwind of the fish and drifted down on the wild scene.

Soon each of us was fast to a fish. Gaffing proved difficult. The wind was gusting twenty or twenty-five miles an hour, the little boat was wallowing in waves at least five feet high, and every move had to be nicely timed. Once a fish was gaffed, we dispatched him with a sharp blow from a short wooden billy.

The blues, which averaged five pounds, put up their usual brilliant fight, sometimes tail-walking and shaking their heads, sometimes leaping horizontally over the water.

We caught them on surface and underwater plugs and on metal jigs such as the Hopkins. Blues also like Alou eels, but their sharp teeth will usually ruin an eel, whether real or artificial, on the first strike.

In the frenzy of feeding, blues cut and slash at the bait, and there is evidence that terns are sometimes crippled or killed by feeding bluefish. Reinfelder has seen a tern's wing floating near bluefish, and he also has picked up a tern with its wing nearly severed.

Shortly before ten we had boated fourteen bluefish, and there were half a dozen large schools of them, each marked by its entourage of birds, feeding within a mile of us, but the seas were running heavier and it seemed advisable to go ashore.

There was no real danger in the open water. The problem was

how to land on the rocky beach in the surf without swamping. We cut the outboard motor and backed into the shore, one man at the oars. With some skill and a lot of luck we managed the beaching without shipping more than a gallon of water.

We gave nine of the fish to a group of anglers on the shore, and two more to a gas station operator near Al's home in Little Rock, so when we arrived at his house to be greeted by his pretty wife, Tommy, and his two young sons we had nothing to show but wet feet and six fillets I had cut from three of the blues at the beach.

Tommy, incidentally, is the only woman I know who can smoke small black cigars without looking foolish.

Argus Never Pointed a Bird, But Became a Good Companion

$\mathbf{A}$rgus the bird dog was an aristocrat. His new master was not, but for thirty of his forty years the man had cherished a dream picture of himself striding through brown meadows and forests of flaming hardwoods after quail or partridge, fine double gun in hand, and a flashy pointer running on before. He believed that he and Argus might, because of a common interest, surmount the differences in their family backgrounds.

The dog was born in October, so that the first fall bird-hunting season of his days was lost. During deer month, Argus watched his master go forth booted and spurred while he was left behind. Seeking some form of useful toil, he slept days and devoted evenings to taking dolls from the little girl's bedroom.

He'd arrange the dolls in a row in front of the fireplace and lie down among them, head up, smiling.

Then spring came. The four feet of snow standing in the woods sagged visibly each day, brooks that would be dry in August roared down the mountains, ice broke up on the river, and several nights each week the dog's master went to the cellar, where he spent hours with bits of feathers and fur and tiny hooks.

Argus always lay beside him and often managed to ruin a squirrel tail or a mallard wing that had fallen to the floor unnoticed.

When the trout fishing began, Argus never understood why he was not allowed in the canoe, so at first he sat on the shore and wept. Later he found comfort in continuous circuits of the pond, slipping and sliding over rocks and stumps, crashing through underbrush, an ever-moving patch of brown and white seen dimly through the green.

The young dog also learned to walk on birch trees that had fallen into the pond, and he sometimes reached the end before he'd topple overboard. Embarrassed at his awkwardness, he did not immediately swim ashore, but clung to the smooth trunk with his front paws, striving desperately to haul himself back up. Other skills he acquired included catching frogs and barking at rising trout.

When the bird-hunting season arrived, the man had not found time to train the dog. Nonetheless, they went afield, and after six days and sixty miles they bagged two partridges, both flushed by the man. Not once that fall did Argus find a bird, and it was clear that he never would.

But before their relationship deteriorated, the two reached an understanding: the dog gave up dolls, the man gave up his dream, and they spent many pleasant winter evenings dozing before the fireplace or tying flies in the cellar.

Ten-Pound Lead Ball
Gets Lure Down to
Lake Michigan Coho

Manistee, Michigan

Lowering a ten-pound lead ball seventy feet into the wind-churned waters of Lake Michigan, Captain Bob Hecht, who keeps his thirty-five-foot Chris-Craft, *Misty II,* at Manistee, promised us a coho salmon.

We soon had four lines overboard as three other balls went the same route. The fishing lines themselves were attached with a quick-release clip to the balls a few feet ahead of the lures. We were trolling at perhaps four miles an hour in 120 to 150 feet of water.

Within fifteen minutes Captain Hecht cried happily, "A good one! A good one! and another!" He was referring to odd-shaped blips, resembling inverted V's, that had appeared on the taper of the Vexilar Sona-Graph installed in the cabin of his boat. A few seconds later a twelve-pound coho, fat, deep-bellied, and silvery, hit one of the lures, shot to the surface, and was boated.

The combination of the electronic report on the captured fish was particularly pleasing to John Uldrich, who is president of Vexilar, Inc., of 1531 East Franklin Avenue, Minneapolis, the firm that manufactures the Sona-Graph. There are various fish-finding sonar units on the market. Uldrich's machine is particularly interesting in that anglers have discovered that certain fish produce unique signals on it. Hecht can, for example, distinguish on the graph between lake trout and coho.

Misty Il's radio was filled with chatter from other charter and sport-fishing boats, and it soon became apparent that most of them were employing a sonar device of some kind to measure water depth and to locate fish.

The reel-like devices that lower the lead ball down into the water on wire line are commonly called downriggers, and there are several models available commercially. In a few hours fishing we caught several more coho, including one of fourteen pounds, and a small lake trout, returning to port in time to fillet several of the smaller salmon.

These we delivered to the chef at the Chippewa Coral Gables Hotel in Manistee with specific suggestions for broiling them. This included brushing with butter, dusting with salt, pepper, dry mustard, and brown sugar, and topping off with a few capers and lemon juice. Served with a good white wine (it could have been a light red wine) they were excellent, although Hecht said that the spring-run fish are superior.

The coho, a West Coast salmon introduced into the lake with brilliant success in the last half-decade, dies after spawning in the fall. The two larger fish we caught already showed some signs of deterioration—their flesh was losing some of its firmness.

A few years ago DDT present in the yolk sac of coho salmon smolt in Lake Michigan seriously hampered hatchery production of the species. DDT, ranging from 9 to 15 parts per million, is present in some mature Lake Michigan coho at present. The federal Food and Drug Administration has set a limit of 5 parts per million as safe for human consumption.

The state of Michigan, which now has what is virtually a total ban of the pesticide, has established 15 parts per million as the upper limit of safety for those who would eat salmon and trout from the lake.

(This column was published in September, 1970.)

Mercury-Contaminated Fish Are Sometimes Safe to Eat

One meal a week of fish taken from most mercury-contaminated waters is probably safe, according to a report in the September *Bulletin* of the Sport Fishing Institute.

The qualifications in the above statement are necessary because, as the institute's Richard Stroud put it in a recent telephone conversation, "anyone who ate fish from highly contaminated waters would be a damn fool."

The federal Food and Drug Administration has set 0.5 milligram of mercury a kilogram (2.2 pounds) of fish flesh as the maximum allowable for human consumption. The institute's suggestion of no more than one meal a week applies to fish containing mercury up to the F.D.A.-permitted maximum.

The institute, whose address is 719 Thirteenth Street, N.W., Washington, D.C. 20005, says "Probably well over 90 per cent of America's inland waters would fail, on detailed sampling of their aquatic life, to yield fish that are contaminated with dangerous quantities of mercury," and adds that few anglers "need fear the occasional eating of small portions of their catches."

To be more specific, S.F.I. says that any angler would have to consume about eighty pounds of mercury-contaminated fish a year before he faced any danger from poisoning. This figure assumes that all the fish consumed contained the maximum amount of mercury allowed by the F.D.A.

The average American freshwater angler, boasting to the contrary, catches about twenty-three pounds of fish annually, and the consumption of commercial fish products (which include both salt and fresh water) by the typical fish-eater is ten to eleven pounds a year.

The danger of serious mercury contamination of fish appears to be largely confined to freshwater lakes and rivers, although it has shown up in some river estuaries in Texas, Georgia, and South Carolina.

In the East, according to S.F.I., only a portion of the St. Lawrence River in Ontario, Lake St. Francis, is contaminated. The Ontario provincial government reports that white bass and walleyed pike from the western end of Lake Erie contain dangerous levels of mercury. Ontario has closed commercial fishing for walleyes in Lake Huron because of mercury contamination.

Some Vermont waters, including Lake Champlain, have yielded fish containing three and four times the permissible concentrations of mercury.

Although the prospect of eating fish contaminated with mercury is not appealing, S.F.I. notes that both humans and fishes are capable of voiding mercury from their systems at the rate of about 0.05 milligram a day. Sweden, whose safety limit is only half as stringent as that of the United States, recommends that an individual limit himself to one meal a week of fish containing more than 0.2 milligram of mercury.

Wisconsin State health authorities recommend the same eating habits for those consuming fish taken from the mercury-contaminated portions of the Wisconsin River.

Mercury is used in many manufacturing processes, including pulp and paper and certain chemical industries, and is frequently discharged into waterways. Mercury poisoning in a human attacks the central nervous system. In the aforementioned conversation, Stroud noted that the phrase "mad as a hatter" may have evolved from damage done to a hatter's brain by the mercury used as a slimicide in the production of felt hats.

(This column was published in October, 1970.)

Tide Moans across the Vast Miles of Ontario's James Bay Region

James Bay, Ontario

Peter Cummins of Old Saybrook, Connecticut, and I sat in the mud in our goose blind, and between us his Chesapeake retriever Beau whimpered and moved nervously, trying to find a dry spot.

It was late afternoon and the sun came out for the first time in a day of rain and gusty winds that died as quickly as they were born.

When the wind dropped we heard a weird, muted murmur, not unlike the sound of a train over a vast distance.

We were listening to the tide coming in. Before us a tidal flat extended for several miles into James Bay, a shimmering expanse of gleaming mud marked with occasional puddles of water or stranded driftwood. For a long time we could not see the approaching water, but the murmuring grew louder—water flowing over miles of tidal flats, swirling into depressions as it moved inland.

Then, perhaps an hour later, we saw the line of water moving at us, sliding swiftly over the flat land, and before it came an incredible profusion of birds: plovers, snipe, sandpipers, teal, mallards, gulls.

The shore birds were tame, often alighting a few feet from us on grassy hummocks. They showed less fear of us than of the ever-present hawks of many species that were everywhere, wheeling low over the land behind us for rodents or sweeping the mud flats for shore birds. One large osprey appeared, but we did not see him catch a fish. (Our guide, Alec Hunter, said "trout" of five pounds and more have been netted in the nearby Moose River.)

The tide moved toward us at amazing speed, nearly half as fast as a man could walk, and crept over out booted feet and up to our knees. We moved our blind back only to be once again surrounded by water that a few hours before had been three miles distant.

With the coming of the tide, water craft appeared. Canoes bearing Cree Indians, or Cree and their guided parties, moved swiftly, driven by outboard motors, through Wavy Creek, which separated us from Shipsands Island; out in the bay, a Hudson's Bay Company barge under tow resumed its southward movement.

One of the canoes pulled ashore a half mile south of us, and the two Cree aboard swiftly erected the light-colored wall tent that is the traditional bush abode for James Bay goose hunts. During our stay these tents (which are translucent), illuminated from the inside by lantern, served as welcome beacons for navigating. In the fog or on a cloudy night it is easy for anyone who has ventured inland to get turned about. There are no prominent landmarks. A man standing a mile away looms up like a tower.

Driftwood is the only fuel available. It rained at least some part of every day during our hunt, and keeping a reasonable supply of dry firewood on hand for our tent stove was difficult. (An ultralight chain saw would be a splendid addition to such an expedition.)

Oyster Mushrooms the Only Thing Two New Hampshire Fishermen Get

Enfield, New Hampshire

Shining flakes of snow slanted down from a small black cloud, melting the instant they touched the wind-ruffled waters of Halfmile Pond.

The northern half of the pond was in shadow, and we—Victor Pomiecko of Claremont, New Hampshire, and I—were cold when the sun was not on us. Halfmile has yielded us many fine brook trout over the last fifteen years, but it was not destined to do so that day. We fished shallow and deep, wet and dry, without a rise, nor did we during our four hours at the pond ever see a fish break water.

From the day after Labor Day until October 15, New Hampshire has a trout season for fly-fishermen only, although this is not limited to the cast fly, and many anglers on larger ponds and lakes use spinning rods to troll flies for trout.

By the end of the first week in October the water in the ponds in the central part of the state has usually cooled into the low 50's and the fish are feeding voraciously on all available forms of aquatic insects plus any of the terrestrial variety that have fallen into the water. But the summer had been long and hot, and the fall unusually mild, and Halfmile was not as cold as it normally is at this time of year.

Halfmile is one of the smaller and more attractive of the state's remote trout ponds and is accessible via a woods road and a trail that leads for a mile through small swamps and forest. Its steep shores are lined with hardwood and softwood trees, and all around the borders of the pond the white trunks of birches slant down into the water. The fallen birches are the work of beavers who have maintained two lodges on the west shore for many years. This fall the lodges were enormous, one of them reaching nearly eight feet above the water, and Vic and I wondered whether this was simply blind devotion to industry or advance information that a long, cold winter lay ahead.

In such ponds trout sometimes benefit from the activities of their furry neighbors, who labor diligently to keep the water level stable. Beavers enter their lodges through underwater passages, and any excess outflow that would expose these passages is quickly plugged. Sometimes beavers raise the level of a natural pond several feet. (They often do this after they have cut down all the choice and edible trees close to the water's edge.) According to New Hampshire fish and game officials, tannic acid from the bark of drowned trees sometimes enters the water in sufficient amounts to kill the trout.

We stopped fishing in midafternoon, wearying of the unrewarding effort. Fifteen years before, we would have cast without pause until dark, but time has blunted our once-keen desire always to catch fish. This is a common syndrome with hunters and fishermen as they grow older: the ritual of the pursuit becomes almost as important as fish or game in the bag.

We did not leave Halfmile empty-handed, however. Beside the trail on the way out Vic found a good-sized clump of oyster mushrooms growing on a young maple, and they found their way into our supper that night. This mushroom, *Pleurotus ostreatus,* is excellent when fried in butter, or it can be dipped in egg batter and cracker crumbs and then fried.

Channel Bass Favorite Prey of Outer Banks Anglers

Nags Head, North Carolina

It was late afternoon but the sun was warm, and I waited far out on a sandbar to cast to the breaking fish.

In the north, Cape Hatteras Light gleamed through the haze, and shore birds and gulls dipped and wheeled in the low-slanting light. The water was also warm, warmer than the air, and the waves, which tumbled erratically over the bar, carried a heavy burden of sand, Sargasso weed, and eel grass.

Frequently dark ruffled patches on the surface of the ocean erupted into thousands of silvery fish: mullet fleeing from small bluefish, and sometimes the blues themselves, burst from the water, pursued by albacore. The shadowy forms of the mullet could be seen in the curl of every wave, suspended momentarily in their watery towers.

As sunset neared, vehicles began to appear, scooting down the side, hard-packed strands bristling with surf rods. Most of these were driven by local anglers, residents of the Outer Banks, coming to fish through twilight for channel bass, also known as red drum.

The red drum bears a superficial resemblance to its more widely scattered cousin, the striped bass, although it is not as deep-bellied as the striper, lacks the striper's lateral lines, and has a relatively small underslung mouth adapted to bottom feeding. The channel bass also carries a dark spot on its tail.

Channel bass, like stripers, are dogged, hard-fighting fish that often go wild just as they are being dragged from the surf. A tired striper will usually lie flat on his side in the wash when pulled from the waves, but the channel bass will often turn and swim on little more than wet sand in an effort to return to the ocean.

On two of our three days of fishing with guide Robert Preston of Nags Head, we caught channel bass averaging about eight pounds. We were bottom fishing, using mullet for bait.

There seems to be no precise designation, but most Outer Banks men call channel bass up to ten pounds puppy drum, fish from ten to twenty pounds yearlings, and those larger, big drum.

Night is a particularly good time to go for drum, but Preston says that fishing must be done without any artificial light. "Drum are amazingly sensitive to light," he says. "A lantern or a car's highlights will scatter a school in seconds."

The other member of our party, Joel Arrington of the North Carolina Department of Development and Conservation, added to Preston's comment: "They are also sensitive to noise or disturbance. If you are casting to a school of them from a boat, you have to keep well off, and often after you've hooked two or three the rest will leave. Yet the drum is such a primitive creature he will hit a lure as he is running away in apparent terror."

"That's right," said Preston. "The drum is like that. Often when caught in a net he will continue to feed on the smaller fish that are trapped with him."

Enchanted Goblin of the Vineyard, the Heath Hen, Is Gone Forever

Wandering through a portion of the so-called Great Plain on Martha's Vineyard Island a few weeks ago, I came to an open space of perhaps an acre where for some reason the gnarled and twisted scrub oaks that cover much of the area could not grow.

Pausing to watch a small doe on the opposite side of the field that was not yet aware of me, I thought of the heath hen, the strange and wonderful bird that completed its journey to oblivion on the Vineyard plains thirty-six years ago.

The heath hen, or Eastern prairie chicken, was once plentiful throughout the East, but by 1839 it existed only on Martha's Vineyard. During that century it was protected from hunters by law on several occasions and was given total protection in the early 1900's.

In 1908 less than sixty birds were still alive, but this number had increased to perhaps two thousand in 1916, when a great fire swept the plain in the spring, catching the females on their nests. In retrospect it is clear that this fire destroyed all chance for survival of the species.

Accurate counts of the birds were aided by its spring mating habits. In April and May the male heath hens gathered in certain open areas on the plain to feed, dance, posture, and make the incredible sounds that stirred the imagination and pens of those who were fortunate enough to hear them.

About the size of a ruffed grouse, the heath hen often made a mournful hooting, a sound one observer said might be duplicated by blowing across the open mouth of a small vial. When flying, it often gave vent to what sounded, when heard in the early morning mists or in the failing light of evening across the vast, storm-buffeted plain, like a burst of demonic laughter.

By 1929 only one bird, a male, survived. It came alone to a field on the farm of James Green in West Tisbury and went through an abbreviated version of the usual mating ritual. In 1930 it appeared again, but omitted any courtship maneuvers and uttered no sound. It came to the same spot once more in the spring of the following year and then was seen no more.

Shortly after this I worked, as a young boy, for Mr. Green. He taught me how to fork hay onto a horse-drawn wagon and how to unload it in the hot, rich-smelling, and mote-filled barn. He taught me how to handle my end of a two-man crosscut saw and he also let me hide in the weathered heath hen observation house at the edge of his field.

I spent many hours in that tiny building, hoping to see or hear the bird whose race had already vanished from the earth, and saw instead crows tumbling down a bright spring sky and sun glistening on wheeling gulls; I heard only the wind in the twisted pitch pines, the rustling and songs of thrushes in the scrub oaks, and the distant hollow roar of the Atlantic, three miles away. The goblins of the enchanted plain were gone forever, and the world was poorer than a boy could know.

Mute Swans Are Beautiful, But They Are a Problem Too

From Massachusetts to Maryland a growing population of mute swans is bringing pleasure to some people and displeasure to others.

These huge feral birds are disliked by many duck hunters who believe, with some justification, that they drive away wild ducks and geese. However, many nonhunters feel that the swans add a touch of grace and beauty to any body of water. The birds are a domestic species gone wild. Many may have descended from swans imported from Europe by Long Island estate owners early in the century.

For six years the Rhode Island Department of Natural Resources has been studying its mute swan colony, which numbered about 550 in 1967, in an effort to determine, among other things, its effect on other waterfowl.

A summary of this work was presented at the Northeast Fish and Wildlife Conference in Bedford, New Hampshire, earlier this year by Charles Willey, a biologist for the department.

The mute swan's zealous guarding of the territory around its nesting site may present more of a problem to waterfowl than the bird's heavy appetite, Willey believes. Although they may share a small body of water with other birds, swans tend to resent intruders. A pair of nesting swans stakes a claim on an area ranging from less than one acre to nearly twelve acres.

An adult mute swan consumes at least 8.4 pounds of wet aquatic vegetation a day. Sometimes this vegetation is not eaten but torn up in the excitement of the nesting ritual. Willey reported that one cob (male swan) so stimulated destroyed a half acre of pickerel weed.

There are usually six to eight eggs in each nest, and swans frequently use the same nesting site for successive years.

The primary natural enemy of the swan appears to be the snapping turtle, which drags the cygnets down and eats them. Bad weather during the incubation period, and disease and parasites, also tend to hold the population in check.

The age a mute swan can reach is a matter for conjecture, but they may live for a half century or more.

Although mute swans are protected by state law in all the states in which they are present, irate hunters have been known to shoot an occasional bird. There is also, Willey said, some illegal traffic in live birds. An adult pair can bring two hundred dollars, he said.

Adult swans can injure children and even adults, Willey said. He cited one instance in which an enraged cob attacked his skiff, and only skillful boat-handling stopped the swan from coming aboard.

(This column was published in February, 1968.)

Leather Belt Gives Final Touch to Knife-Sharpening Ritual

The bare spot on my left forearm is the place where I test my knives. If they shave me, they are properly sharp.

Keeping a hunting knife, jackknife, or kitchen knife keen is a relatively simple matter, and the tools needed are a sharpening steel, a combination oilstone (smooth grit on one side, coarse on the other), and a razor strop. If you cannot find a razor strop, an old leather belt will do.

Knives just purchased are rarely sharp, and sometimes their edges are so blunt that preliminary thinning with a file is in order. After filing, the knife should go on the oilstone's coarse side, then on the smooth side. Putting a few drops of light oil or water on the stone is helpful.

When sharpening, always draw the knife toward you, against the edge of the blade, the full length of the stone. The angle at which one holds the knife against the stone is important; 35 degrees is about right. The file and the coarse grit remove excess metal and nicks. The smooth side of the stone begins to give the knife a good edge, and this should be followed with the belt or razor strop, using a barber's technique.

If fifteen or twenty strops on each side of the blade fail to make it sharp enough to shave your forearm, repeat the oilstone-strop routine. High-speed grinding wheels should be avoided. Unless one is unusually skilled, the temper will be drawn from the blade, making it virtually useless. If you must try a grinding wheel, dip the blade in water frequently to cool it off. Of course, if you happen to have an old-fashioned, foot-powered grindstone in your dooryard, it would do the job perfectly.

The sharpening steel is a handy tool and will keep a blade functional for a long time, but I have never been able to achieve a shaving edge with a steel alone.

Although there have been major advances in metallurgy in the last few years, many outdoorsmen still favor a carbon steel hunting knife, and they feel the same way about kitchen knives. The early stainless steel blades, which appealed to housewives because they did not rust or stain, were soft as butter and would not hold an edge. There have been, I am informed, great improvements in the manufacture of stainless steel knives recently, but I see no reason to abandon the time-tested carbon steel products.

Buying and sharpening kitchen knives is one function that a man's wife will readily assign to him. If you are in doubt as to the proper tools for carving meat and bread, peeling potatoes, or filleting fish, visit your neighborhood butcher shop and fish market and ask the professionals.

One device to be avoided is the electric carving knife. None can deny that it does the job, but so would a chain saw. The ritual of carving a prime roast or a plump turkey is destroyed by the chattering of the shiny blades. No man of spirit would allow such an abomination in his home.

When Wine Freezes,
It Is Time for
Anglers to Return Home

$\mathbf{M}$ore than a decade ago a friend and I hiked to the top of a small mountain in New Hampshire to ice fish for pickerel.

We wore snowshoes and pulled our gear on a toboggan over four feet of snow. The day was cold, 20 below zero, and the wind was gusting up to thirty miles an hour.

After reaching the top, we built a windbreak from an old tarpaulin, lit a fire, and chopped half a dozen holes through the ice. Before an hour had passed, we learned that we couldn't fish. The holes became covered with a skim of ice and drifting snow faster than we could keep them open.

Resigned to this, we retired to the fire and found that a bottle of wine we had brought with us had congealed into unpourable slush. This more than anything else sent us down the mountain. If wine froze, we reasoned, so would we.

I do not recall, however, that we were ever dangerously cold, even though we wore only mediumweight wool hunting jackets. The explanation was that the exertion required in climbing and cutting firewood and ice had kept us warm. Yet it is possible for a deer hunter out in weather only a little below freezing to be absolutely miserable. The winter hunter's problem is that the clothing that keeps him warm while he is moving through the woods does not usually suffice when he stands still along a deer trail.

Deer hunters often sit or move very slowly until they start to shiver, then walk at a fairly rapid pace to a new location.

Perspiration and subsequent loss of body heat is a problem for the winter foot traveler, and he should avoid it. Ventilating net underwear, with mesh openings at least three eighths of an inch square, goes a long way toward keeping body moisture out of one's clothing. Also, before perspiring one should remove his hat and open or loosen outer clothing so excess heat can be carried away.

A hat or a stocking cap is essential to the winter outdoorsman's well-being. The head is the only portion of your body where the blood supply is not reduced when you become chilled. It therefore follows that your hat should come off when you are in danger of sweating and go on when you are fighting the cold.

Boots should be large enough to accommodate two pairs of wool socks and still fit loosely, and if the boots are not insulated there should be room for felt insoles.

Dressing for duck hunting is a different proposition. The sport is basically sedentary, whether one is crouched on spray-drenched rocky islets in Long Island Sound in December waiting for bluebills to come to the decoys, or kneeling behind blinds of brush on the shores of James Bay, Ontario, calling to blue geese. Waterfowlers may pile on clothing, and the only worry will be whether they can move their arms well enough to shoulder a gun.

Amateur Guide Leads Editor to His First Bluefish in Surf

Katama Opening, Martha's Vineyard, Massachusetts

A night rain had fallen, blackening the asphalt road to Katama Beach, but the sky was clear except in the east, where a dark cloud obscured the rising sun.

We met at the end of the road, Robert Manning and I, and he joined me in my jeep for the two-and-one-half-mile trip down the beach to the cut where Katama Bay opens into the ocean. It was five thirty, but Manning, who is the editor of *Atlantic Monthly*, was remarkably chipper. The sea was calm and there were no signs of terns or fish feeding, only occasional bands of herring gulls congregated above the tide line, knots of seaweed, dunnage planks, and frequent windrows of blue mussels thrown up by storms.

The ride to Katama Opening is much longer than it used to be. In recent years the opening has moved steadily east along the shore and is now chewing at the west end of Chappaquiddick Island. The root systems of scrub oaks and pitch pines have slowed but not stopped this erosion, and the gnarled snags torn from Chappaquiddick lie strewn along the shore.

Two four-wheel-drive camping vehicles were at the opening when we arrived, and one man was busily working the water with a popping plug.

The previous evening I had told Manning that we probably would not find striped bass but that there was some chance of catching medium-sized bluefish. Giant blues, fish to eighteen pounds, were off Katama and Chappaquiddick earlier this summer, but they moved offshore in July and August, as is their custom. The big fellows will return sometime in early or mid-September.

For more than an hour the three of us fished steadily but with no results. There were shoals of small spearing in the opening, ideal forage for bluefish, and although they flared out of the water from time to time, there was no evidence that blues were chasing them.

I was grateful for the time of no fish, for I was testing a new spinning reel, the big Garcia 498, which has a manual pickup. With the typical open face spinning reel, the bail automatically picks up the line. A manual pickup requires that the angler himself engage the line with the pickup finger of the reel. In a half-hour I had learned the proper technique, which involves stopping the outflowing line with one's fingers just before the lure hits the water, and engaging it with the pickup before there is any slack.

By 7 A.M. several terns picked a few bait fish from the east-running tide before us, and shortly thereafter we began to take bluefish in the three-to-five-pound class.

By eight o'clock Manning and I had caught five blues and lost three more. And we left, having promised our respective spouses we would be home early.

It had been a pleasant morning, made doubly so by Manning's obvious delight. He had, by the way, caught his blues on a one-handed spinning rod and ten-pound-test line.

"It was my first time at surf-fishing and the first time I've ever seen anything caught from the surf," he said, sweet words to an amateur guide.

Muskellunge Give Anglers a Lesson in Humility

Cass Lake, Minnesota

Each year as a form of penance, a lesson in humility, anglers should go in quest of muskellunge.

One may be a master of the fly rod, a veteran surf caster, or an old hand with fighting chairs and billfish, but this means virtually nothing in muskie country, where incredible patience and a minor form of madness are essential to success. Some men, for example, have fished for muskies for ten years with no reward.

The muskie is a large freshwater fish (the rod-and-reel record for him is sixty-nine pounds) whose sporadic feeding habits and surly disposition make him difficult to catch.

At the International Muskie Tournament last weekend at Cass Lake, two hundred contestants fished two and a half days and landed five muskies. The winner of the event was Edward Peterka of St. Paul, Minnesota, with a 28-pound 4-ounce fish; second was Walter Roeker of Jamesville, Minnesota, 20 pounds, and third was Gil Hamm of St. Paul, whose muskie weighed 19 pounds 8 ounces.

It was altogether fitting that Hamm was among the top three, for he is the president of Muskies, Inc., a private group of muskie devotees laboring to improve the fishing for the species in the state.

Muskies, Inc., along with the Cass Lake Sportsmen's Club and the Minnesota Department of Tourism, sponsored the tournament. The first prize was a fifteen-foot Crestliner muskie boat.

Wisconsin, Minnesota, New York, and Michigan are the nation's top muskie states, with the record fish coming from the St. Lawrence River in New York State.

Common lures for muskies are large plugs, spoons, and bucktails. Live bait is also used. The most popular muskie reel appears to be one of the Garcia 6,000 series, and rods are relatively short and stiff. The minimum strength line most guides recommend is twenty pounds, although some spinning gear testing as light as fifteen pounds is used.

Our four-man party included John Uldrich, Robert Knutson, and Jack Connor, all of Minneapolis, with Robert Reed of Cass Lake as guide. Uldrich and Knutson are partners in Vexilar Engineering, Inc., of Minneapolis, manufacturers of Sound-Off Sonar, an electronic fish-finder and depth-sounder, and Zonar, an electronic water temperature and depth gauge. Connor is a retired Minneapolis newspaperman.

Backed by Reed's knowledge of the Lake and the Vexilar devices, we were bubbling with confidence the night before the tournament opened, even noting with pleasure that our station wagon had a trailer hitch with which we could pull the first prize home.

(This column was published in September, 1969.)

Angler Resolves He'll Return As a Reincarnated Muskellunge

Cass Lake, Minnesota

It is only proper that as a man approaches the half-century mark his thoughts turn to immortality.

Casting idly for muskellunge along Cass Lake's western shore (in an estimated two thousand casts I had raised, but not hooked, one fish), I resolved that I would endeavor to be reincarnated as a muskie.

I would, I thought, quickly grow to world-record size, anything over seventy pounds, reside in Cass Lake, and live for twenty years, devoting my efforts to exasperating the idiotic anglers who attempted to catch me.

As a former human, I would know that the spinner and bucktail rig or swimming plugs are generally the most effective for muskies, and would therefore make great, showy rushes at all other lures, ignoring the favorites. (Of the nine muskies caught by 243 anglers in the recently completed two-and-one-half-day Cass Lake tournament, five were taken on bucktails and four on underwater plugs, the Cisco Kid and the Pikie Minnow. The winning fish, weighing thirty-eight pounds, was caught by R. J. Stacy of Osseo, Minnesota.)

Plunging deeper into my daydream, I would also, I thought, make frequent follows right up to the boat, sometimes swirling under it at the last minute, sometimes pulling up short with my head and eyes above water, for nothing rattles an angler more than a muskie's steady glare, unless it is his gleaming, snarling head flinging a rejected lure skyward.

And if, I thought, I should tire of this play, if the steady plop of lures in the water above me or their gleaming, writhing, jerking passage past me should no longer be inspirational, and the look of wild frustration on an angler's face no longer bring pleasure, I would sacrifice myself to Gil Hamm of St. Paul, Minnesota.

No one but Hamm should catch me, for this smiling, affable man has dedicated all his spare time and energy to improving the lot of my species. As president of Muskies, Inc. (1708 University Avenue, St. Paul), Hamm has developed an organization that among other things now maintains its own hatchery, where young muskies are raised and then transplanted into Minnesota lakes.

Half of the registration proceeds for the Cass Lake tournament are turned over to Muskies, Inc., and the money will be used to stock twelve-inch muskellunge in Cass and the surrounding lakes fished during the tournament. The cost of raising a muskie to twelve inches in length is two dollars.

I emerged from my fantasy to find that night was settling on the lake. My fishing companions sat silently in the boat, waiting for me to stop casting. A bald eagle slanted down toward his huge nest in a towering pine, a loon screamed across the dark waters, three crows tumbled past the failing light of the western sky, and it was time to leave.

(This column was published in September, 1970.)

Girl Friend Changes the Life of an Ancient, Paunchy Hound

West Tisbury, Massachusetts

Mist was wreathed in the valley, the morning sun had not yet topped the gnarled pines, and louder than the muted roar of the surf on the South Shore of the Vineyard three miles away was the distant voice of a hound giving chase to a cottontail rabbit in the scrub oaks.

That a hound was chasing a rabbit in that damp October dawn was not remarkable, but that the hound was Bingo was almost miraculous.

Bingo joined our family in midsummer, wandering in out of the night—a paunchy, half-blind, half-deaf, half-beagle, half-basset, who was, by a dog's standards, an octogenarian.

Despite his physical shortcomings, my two daughters, aged eleven and seven, fell in love with him. He had, they pointed out, a charming disposition and was always eager to please. They fed and groomed him; they plucked bloated wood ticks from his grayish coat. They tried to induce him to romp with them, but all he could muster was a few ragged hops before his emphysema and excess weight pulled him down.

Each night he slept by the fireplace; the sound of his labored breathing filled the room, and it seemed certain, although the girls would not admit it, that he was deep in senility.

Then, six weeks ago, Bingo was given a companion, a peppery female puppy whose mother, a purebred springer spaniel, had dallied in the bracken with a Labrador retriever. At first Bingo merely endured the noise and excitement the puppy created, frequently leaving the house or the yard to avoid her attempts at play.

Then, slowly, a transformation took place. The old dog's coat began to shine, his first faltering attempts at romping turned into full-fledged gallops. He began to roll on the ground with the pup, snarling at her in mock anger when she pulled his ears, and at night, when he thought no one was looking, he washed her with his tongue.

He no longer growled at her when they ate, but stood aside until she had finished, even allowing her to eat from his dish if she chose. During the day he made sure that she did not wander from the yard and limited his own excursions to early morning before she awakened.

When she had to be taken to the veterinarian's to have her distemper shots, he insisted on going with her.

Then, after six weeks, with sight and hearing improved, his paunch almost gone, and a spring in his stride, he ventured into the woods and ran a rabbit, something he probably hadn't done for years.

Telling Bingo's story to a gaggle of middle-aged matrons, Bingo's master attempted to advance the thesis that the equivalent of a young pup in the life of an aging human male might produce the same results, but he was quickly snarled down.

Off-Islanders Bring New Techniques to Striper Fishing

Menemsha, Massachusetts

Two outlanders, off-islanders from New York State, conquered Martha's Vineyard striped bass last week.

Their methods were unorthodox by Vineyard standards, which only reinforces a basic rule of angling: never get into a rut; remember to experiment when conventional techniques fail.

Hurtling around the island in a nineteen-foot Mako powered by a 105-horsepower Chrysler outboard, Al Reinfelder of Little Neck and Lou Palma of Douglaston, Queens, took fish wherever they went, including many over thirty pounds and one over forty. Their host was a Vineyarder, H. K. Bramhall, Jr., of the *Saltwater Sportsman* magazine.

Reinfelder and Palma, former owners of the Alou tackle company, which produced the plastic Alou eel and bait tail, recently sold their business to the Garcia Corporation. Reinfelder is now a lure designer for Garcia, and was on the Vineyard testing a new product.

The first bit of unorthodoxy practiced by the two occurred off the rocky rough and tumble of the North Shore. Failing to take fish by casting surface plugs from a boat close to the beach, the usual technique, they retreated several hundred yards out into Vineyard Sound and promptly raised and caught big fish in more than twenty feet of water with the same lures.

"That," said Bramhall later, "simply isn't done."

On subsequent days, also off the North Shore, they went to work with the lure they were testing, a device with wire spreader arms sporting five pieces of red surgical tubing, each carrying a hook. (Montauk, Long Island, skippers have been using surgical tubing rigs for several years, but no major tackle firm is producing them.) Dragging these rigs behind the Mako on 100 to 150 feet of wire line in fifteen to forty feet of water, we took three stripers of twenty to thirty pounds in an hour and lost several more.

A bright sun shone on a flat sea that afternoon, and no bait fish or stripers were visible, yet with the Mako's Ross depth recorder we found both, trolled through them, and often hooked bass a short time after we had seen the "spikes" that marked their presence on the depth-recorder chart.

Toward the end of the day Reinfelder hooked something substantial. "It's a hummer!" he cried happily as the striper raced northeast toward the mainland and Woods Hole. It was a hummer, a forty-four-pound striped bass that was deftly gaffed by Palma six minutes after it had been hooked.

The following morning Palma and Reinfelder returned to the spot and hooked a very large fish, probably a striper, which they fought for fifteen minutes before losing. Reinfelder was not depressed, however, for the big fish he had taken the day before was occupying first place in the boat division of the Martha's Vineyard striped bass and bluefish derby.

The Nymphs and Their Consorts Have Left the Beach to the Anglers

West Tisbury, Massachusetts

The hour before dawn was black, a cold northwest wind helped to flatten the rolling combers, and when the sun rose it no longer shone, as it has all summer, on bright sails and beach umbrellas.

Summer was gone. The nymphs and their consorts had departed, leaving the great stretch of Martha's Vineyard Island's South Beach to a few patient fisherman with their long surface rods.

Most of the fishermen had gone also, but a few remained even though the Vineyard's striped bass and bluefish derby had ended a few days before. (The largest striper caught weighed 51 pounds 6 ounces and was taken by Serge de Somov of Hampton Bays, Long Island; the largest blue was 18 pounds 11 ounces, caught by Douglas Gingras of Vineyard Haven.)

The derby, part of the Vineyard scene for more than a quarter of a century and the major event of the year for island anglers, has encountered some resistance from landowners who object to loss of solitude, violation of No Trespassing signs, and the vehicular traffic over the dunes. But for the most part, it has been remarkably free from this sort of trouble.

We were fishing at the Tisbury Great Pond opening, a man-made

176

channel, which fills in from time to time, connecting the pond to the ocean. The opening, in years past dug by men with shovels and hoes, had been made by a bulldozer the day before. Schools of bait fish, crabs, and eels were swept out to sea, attracting the stripers, and among them were small bluefish, or snappers, and a large number of tropical fish of the jack family. The snappers and jacks had been trapped in the pond since early summer, when onshore winds closed the opening, and they undoubtedly raced south, for their departure was long overdue.

During my first morning at the opening I watched my brother take two stripers, one about twelve pounds, the other about twenty-five, while I hooked and lost three fish. The second morning, learning that my brother's fish had been feeding on the young bluefish that had not managed to escape, I went forth with a dozen snappers I had caught in the pond before it was opened, using them for bait.

Dawn rose red as it had the day before. A huge flock of bluebills, perhaps a thousand, rose from the pond, passed over me, and swept out to sea. A dozen Canada geese flew low over the ocean, preceded by an equal number of brant.

I fished for two hours without a hit, then out of that bright dawn a lean and smiling fisherman, H. K. Bramhall, Jr., of Edgartown, walked up behind me and asked if I would like a thirty-five-pound striper he had caught at 4 A.M., the only fish taken at the opening that morning.

His generosity ended my endeavor for the day and for the season. It was, I felt, a proper time to stop. The nights had grown cold, waterfowl were on the move, and in the hardwood forests of the North Woods a grouse flew through a slant of golden light.

"Raccoon" Takes Wing
in the Shape of a
West Virginia Turkey

Marlinton, West Virginia

If R. Wayne Bailey had told me that wild turkeys appeared to be almost black when viewed suddenly in the woods, I might not have missed my shot.

The western wind was a wild torrent in the tall hardwoods, three thousand feet up Tea Creek Mountain in east-central West Virginia, when three hen turkeys leaped from a cluster of blackberry bushes about thirty-five yards away.

I remember seeing a portion of one of them and thinking that it was a raccoon. This notion was spoiled when the creature began to fly. Awakening to reality, I swung on the bird, which was then clearing the tops of the trees forty-five yards away, and fired. It did not fall, nor did it falter, and I was so chagrined I forgot to fire the second barrel.

Bailey, meanwhile, was having a similar experience. Initially, he had a slight edge over me in that he could tell a turkey from a raccoon, but the right barrel of his double gun failed to fire, and when he got around to pulling the other trigger he was so unnerved that he also missed.

"That," he said, "was poor shooting. Why didn't you fire sooner?"

"I thought it was a raccoon," I replied.

He nodded sagely, as if he had heard such an excuse a hundred times before, his lean, tanned face showing no emotion.

"Those were hens," he said. "Gobblers are much darker."

My introduction to wild-turkey hunting had begun a few hours before. It was not yet dawn when we entered the forest at the foot of the mountain, and in the cold dark we removed our hunting boots and socks to wade the icy creek that crosses the trail to the summit.

"It hurts while you're doing it, but it feels wonderful afterward," said my companion as we rubbed our aching feet on the opposite shore.

Bailey, a tall, spare West Virginia native, is director of forest-game research for the Division of Wildlife in the state's Department of Natural Resources. He is one of the department's foremost wild-turkey authorities, and as one might expect, an excellent turkey hunter and wing shot.

Although he is in his early fifties, Bailey is a hard man to follow through the mountains. He lopes over the rugged terrain with deceptive ease and never seems to tire.

Obviously distressed by our poor marksmanship, he had another trial to endure. Later in the day we put up a flock of about thirteen turkeys, and one of them, an old hen, split off from the main flock.

"Wonderful," he said, "she will be vulnerable to calling. She'll want to rejoin the others."

We snuggled into hiding places fifty yards apart on the mountain, and in twenty minutes, using a box-type call, Bailey lured the turkey to within twenty yards before it spotted him and went aloft.

Because the bird jumped before he expected it to, Bailey missed his first shot. He still had plenty of time and an easy wing shot, but as before, his shotgun misfired and the dark, majestic bird sailed into the valley three thousand feet below.

Shark Steaks Nothing to Sneeze At, Says Rhode Island Researcher

Narragansett, Rhode Island

I know a fellow who prefers a nice mako shark steak to swordfish," said John G. Casey. "I'm not an enthusiastic fish-eater, but mako and dogfish (a species of shark), for example, are very tasty. I had two students here one summer who went through 110 pounds of white shark steaks."

Casey, acting director of the Narragansett Marine Gamefish Laboratory, is convinced that sharks are a significant United States fisheries resource, a resource that is currently neglected.

In Japan, Europe, and Africa hundreds of thousands of tons of shark are consumed annually. Commercial landings in the United States are about six or seven million pounds annually. Total United States fish landings run about five billion pounds annually.

To this writer's knowledge, few, if any, of the shark steaks or fillets retailed for human consumption in the United States are labeled shark. Although some people might turn up their noses at shark meat, most Americans who served in the European Theater during World War II probably didn't realize that the fish of England's famous fish and chips was usually dogfish or school shark.

Casey, who has directed a shark research program since 1961, says all sharks found off the northeastern coast of the United States are edible, with mako, porbeagle, thresher, and dogfish considered the best for the table.

To quote from his *Anglers' Guide to Sharks* (which covers those species commonly found from Maine to Chesapeake Bay): "The meat can be boiled, fried, broiled or chowdered, but it should be cooked as soon as possible. Cured, the meat is excellent, whether smoked, salted or kippered.

"Fresh mako, hammerhead, small dusky and dogfish are good eating, particularly when cooked in sauces or with vegetables and other meats. These sharks have a distinctive flavor, milder than some of the more common food fishes."

This booklet, which also contains a shark identification guide, is available from the Superintendent of Documents, Government Printing Office, Washington, D.C. 20402, for twenty-five cents.

The life cycle of most sharks is still a mystery. The female of most species carries her pups from eight to twelve months.

(The spiny dogfish, an exception to the general rule, has a gestation period of nearly two years. A few sharks lay eggs or carry eggs until they are hatched.)

From two to sixty pups, depending upon the species, are born. They are usually about two feet long and are ready to forage for themselves.

The average newborn shark thus escapes the massive mortality common to most fish, who must grow from tiny eggs. Most sharks are slow-growing. Some species may live as long as twenty years, reaching sexual maturity at ten.

Cape Cod Quail Are Fleet, But Hunters Harvest a Few

Falmouth, Massachusetts

This is a land of gnarled scrub oaks and pitch pines, of cranberry bogs and brown meadows, and here and there a tall white pine, whose feathery top streams before the prevailing southwest wind like the hair of a running girl.

In these meadows and oaks and pines are quail, pheasant, and ruffed grouse, although the latter is present in limited numbers, and riding in the back of the station wagon with Elsie "L. C." Smith beside me, I wondered how we would fare on our first hunt together. Elsie, to be charitable, is in late middle age, but her lines are trim and smooth and she has lost none of her style: they literally don't make them like her anymore, and I had been delighted to find her several months before.

Elsie is the perfect quail gun, a 20-gauge, side-by-side double 26-inch barrels, bored improved cylinder in the left barrel and open cylinder in the right.

"In the hands of the right man she should be great," I thought as we dismounted from the station wagon and waited while Bill Fitzpatrick of Marstons Mills unleashed his English setter bitch, Rocket.

I had explained to Bill, a bird-hunting enthusiast who is employed by the Massachusetts Division of Marine Fisheries, and to Ted Vincent of Westport, Massachusetts, outdoor writer for the New Bedford (Massachusetts) *Standard-Times,* that Elsie and I had never been afield together, thereby providing an excuse for a possibly inept performance.

Racing across the meadows of the Crane Wildlife Management Area in the chill mists of early morning, the eager Rocket quickly found a covey and froze into a beautiful point.

Vincent and I moved in, the quail exploded, Vincent fired and missed, and I did not fire at all. The twisted branch of a scrub oak had suddenly jumped between me and the bird I had picked out.

This happened twice again, then on a fast, crossing shot to the right, Elsie and I got a quail, although it did take two shots. Twice more in the next hour I connected on quail, although neither bird was a clean kill. I had spent too much time getting on target, and the shots were long.

Vincent then picked up his first quail after thrashing through briars and scrub oak to get to the pointing dog. The birds in this particular covey were apparently weary, for they scampered through the undergrowth ahead of the panting Vincent for several yards before flushing.

Neither Vincent nor I shot our limit of five birds that morning, and he, lacking my excuse, resorted to an old subterfuge.

"I'm really a conservationist at heart," he said. "I love to shoot at the clouds and watch the birds go by."

Old-Fashioned Dutch Oven
Versatile Outdoor Utensil

There is probably no single piece of outdoor cooking equipment as versatile as the Dutch oven, yet those skilled in its use are rare indeed.

The Dutch oven is a flat-bottomed, heavily built pot made of cast iron, or more recently, cast aluminum. The bottom of the pot has three short legs, and the heavy, close-fitting lid is flanged so hot coals may be piled on it without falling off.

A Dutch oven can be used to bake bread and biscuits, to fry meat and bacon, to cook beans and tasty stews, and to roast fowl and meats.

In my cellar is a sixteen-inch-diameter Dutch oven, which weighs, I think, about fifteen pounds. I use it on camping trips if it can be taken to the campsite by jeep or boat, for it is too heavy for back-packing. Its usual function in camp is to cook the evening meal while I am away for the day. I build a fire in a pit and sear a roast in the Dutch oven. When the fire burns down I remove some of the coals.

The oven goes into the fire hole with the roast, seasoning, water, carrots, onions, and a few potatoes. The lid is loaded with the remaining coals, and the whole affair covered with earth. This is done after breakfast, and there is always a hot meal awaiting at sunset when I return from fishing or hunting.

When I bought my oven, no text on its use was available. Now Don Holm, wildlife editor of the Portland (Oregon) *Oregonian,* has published his *Old-Fashioned Dutch Oven Cookbook,* and the lack is remedied. Holm's book (Caxton Printers, Ltd., Caldwell, Idaho, 106 pages, illustrated, $3.95) has many excellent recipes for Dutch oven cookery and also explores the history of the Dutch oven in America from Colonial times to the present.

Holm has a chapter on sourdough baking, including the rituals one may pursue to make his own sourdough "starter," and there is sound advice on smoking fish and game, and on the preparation of jerky and pemmican.

The large and heavy Dutch ovens are best suited for those who are going into the wilds on horseback or by canoe or boat, but some of the previously mentioned lightweight aluminum models are not too much for the enterprising woodsman who carries his all on his back. There is a list of firms that manufacture Dutch ovens in Holm's book.

One can, if local ordinances permit, practice Dutch oven cooking in his own back yard, and certain foods, including breads, can be baked in an ordinary fireplace.

This is an excellent, honest, informative book, one that would make a good Christmas present for the outdoorsman who enjoys campfire cooking and who would like to gain skill in the use of the remarkably useful but neglected Dutch oven.

The Lowly, Creeping Conch Subject of Rhode Island Study

A pretty young marine biologist of Rhode Island's Department of Natural Resources, Mrs. Rosalind Greene Butziger, has devised a means of marking conches so that she may trace their underwater habits.

Empty conch shells are often found tossed up on Atlantic beaches. Children are advised to hold them to their ears so they may hear "the sound of the sea" purported to be trapped within the shell. Conches were once used by offshore dory fishermen to signal the mother ship when fog set in, but the art of conch-blowing appears to have passed away.

The conch, or more properly, the whelk, that Mrs. Butziger is studying is the channeled whelk of Narragansett Bay. There is commercial fishing for this gastropod in the bay from April or May through November. Fishermen receive four dollars to five dollars a bushel for them. They are sold, in the main, to food processors. Ground whelk can be used as a base for macaroni and spaghetti sauce or as a chowder.

The report on Mrs. Butziger's work with whelks was given at the recent Northwest Wildlife Conference in Bedford, New Hampshire.

Whelks are predators and scavengers and will eat quahogs, oysters, and clams. They also steal bait from lobster pots.

For many years there has been a limited market for whelks along the Eastern seaboard, supported mostly by first-generation Italian-Americans who knew a good conch when they saw one. Several years ago there was a whelk fisherman known as King Conch who often put into Menemsha Harbor on Martha's Vineyard.

The whelks are trapped in pots that resemble those of the lobster man. However, the conch pot has no funnel. It is a rectangular box with an opening on top. The conches crawl up the side of the box and drop through the opening to get at the bait, which is placed within.

Whelks emerge tiny, but fully formed, from strings of horny egg cases familiar to any visitor to our summer beaches. Sometimes the whelks have not escaped from the case, and it is always a source of delight to the amateur naturalist when he first opens one of these tough sacs to find dozens of the minute whelks within.

Marine biologists have speculated that it might be possible to trap the whelks from prime quahog, clam, and oyster grounds and transplant them to areas where they would do no damage to those species.

Mrs. Butziger and her coworkers have marked and tagged one thousand whelks thus far. A disk is fastened to the shell with epoxy cement and a line of colored epoxy cement is painted around the lip of the shell.

It is the fleshy foot of the whelk that is eaten. The viscera should be discarded and the horny extremity of the foot removed. Whelks can be boiled in the shell and the meat ground, as previously mentioned, for spaghetti sauce or chowder, or perhaps as a stuffing with spices and bread crumbs.

However, one may also break the creature's shell to gain access to the uncooked meat, which may be sliced in steaks no more than three eighths of an inch thick, beaten with a rolling pin or mallet, and fried.

(This column was published in January, 1968.)

Ammunition No Necessity During Ontario Partridge Hunt

Williamsburg, Ontario

After three days of chasing Hungarian partridges in Dundas County, I am the rightful owner of a thirty-five-dollar Province of Ontario small-game hunting license, which I probably will not use again before its expiration date, and there are no birds in my game bag.

I am, however, pleased to report that I fired only one shell. To hunt three days and fire once is an achievement. The next step would be to eschew ammunition altogether.

The Hungarian partridges of the dairy country of Dundas County are not, I should hasten to say, a myth, for I have seen them and held them in my hand. They are covered with feathers and are about two thirds the size of a ruffed grouse.

The four birds I held in my hand were shot by John Falk of White Plains, or our guide, Allan Baker.

In addition to the unfortunate four, I saw fifty or sixty other huns, as they are commonly called, usually from vast distances. One of the birds shot by Baker was scratched out of a covey of ten that flushed wild when we were at least fifty-five yards away. It was then that I understood why Baker was armed with a full-choke, 12-gauge Remington more suitable for ducks than upland birds.

188

Despite this, Falk and I clung to our trim little Model 101 Winchester 20-gauge over and unders, bored modified and improved cylinder.

The first day we saw no huns at all, but went forth again the following morning resolving to pursue them in fields of tall corn, where Baker thought they might be lurking. It was on the edge of a cornfield that we took two birds from a covey of about thirteen. Marking the flight of the survivors, we crossed a half-mile of meadow and seven barbed-wire fences to the opposite edge of the corn. At that point Baker made the aforementioned long shot.

The third and last day we quickly limbered up on twenty-two fences, several miles of stubbled grain fields, and occasional sorties into the standing corn, where the gray, claylike soil sticking to the bottom of our boots soon made us three inches taller.

Leaving the corn, we spotted twelve huns dancing and dusting on a gravel road. They saw the whites of our eyes at 150 yards and flew into a just-cut grain field. We followed, with one of Falk's two English setters ranging on ahead. They flew again when we were sixty yards away, but one remained behind and flushed when we were a few yards away. He was shot.

Nearly a mile away, still chasing the same covey, I fired my only shot. In a narrow roadway between some small trees and bushes, the birds rose quickly, but quicker yet was my little gun. There was a satisfying explosion. The branch of a young maple, shattered by my shot charge, hung askew. Several crimson leaves fluttered down, and the huns flew on.

In summation, the hun is a splendid, often spooky, fast-flying game bird. His numbers in Dundas County may be down slightly from last year, but hunting will improve in a few weeks when the tall corn, which provides cover for the birds, is harvested.

Prolific Oysters Start Life
As Males, Then Change Sex

It is somehow fitting that the oyster, a creature so vulnerable in childhood, has clothed its maturity in a horny myth of inaccessibility.

The East Coast oyster, *Crassostrea virginica,* always female in adulthood, can release five million eggs during one spawning. An oyster usually starts life as a male, then in middle age declines the gambit and becomes female. The young male release sperm that joins with the unfertilized eggs. At this stage of life, hordes of the free-swimming, naked oysters are devoured by tiny marine crustaceans.

Later, when the young bivalves have settled down and started to build a shell, crabs and bottom fish continue the depredation. Also, millions of baby oysters find no suitable spot to call home, and, swept to and fro by tidal currents, eventually sink to the bottom, where they are suffocated by silt or mud.

A year or two after birth, the oysters that survive are ready for man. Incidentally, the age of any oyster can be roughly estimated by the lines on its shell, like growth rings on a tree or wrinkles on a woman's face.

Now that we are well into the months of R's, oysters are legitimate prey for those who frequent seacoast areas.

Oyster beds are found in the tidewater ponds and estuaries of the East and often may be plundered at low tide by those equipped with no more than a potato fork and resistance to cold water. A bottle of wine is an acceptable kit item for an oyster hunter. If you open an occasional bivalve and wash it down with a stiff slug of port, you can often forget the tide as it creeps from knee to thigh and beyond.

When gathering oysters for a stew, don't pass up the huge, gnarled dowagers, but if you plan to serve them on the half shell choose their smaller, shapelier husbands—they are easier to open and look pretty on a plate.

Many oyster gatherers have been stopped short of success by the creature's formidable exterior. Others, driven wild by the thought of the succulent delight within, have attacked them with hammers, but this behavior is irresponsible.

A heavy pair of gloves and a good oyster knife are the basic shucking tools. Place the oyster deep side down on a working surface with its hinged end away from you. Press the heel of your left hand down on top of the oyster, holding it firmly, and with your right hand insert the knife between the two shells. Work the knife across the oyster under the top shell and pivot it back and forth until you sever the adductor muscle. Flip the top shell free, cut the adductor loose from the bottom shell, and the act is completed.

Oysters do not, like wine, improve with storage, but you can keep them in a cool place for a week or two with no ill effects, opening them as desire and enterprise command. A century ago seacoast dwellers gathered oysters in the fall and stored them in damp, cool root cellars throughout the winter.

191

New Hampshire's Wary Animal Is Called a Species of Coyote

Boscawen, New Hampshire

There is a shy animal roaming the forests of New Hampshire that is larger than the Plains coyote and smaller than the gray wolf.

He has not yet been named, although the people who have been closest to him believe he is fundamentally "a coyote that was modified a long time ago." He is, they say, not a recent hybrid dog-coyote.

This is the judgment of Mrs. Helenette Silver, who with her husband, Walter, has just completed six years of behavioral and breeding studies of the animals. The Silvers, who are biologists for the New Hampshire Fish and Game Department, literally took these animals into their own home during the study period and developed a deep affection for their shy, intelligent charges.

The study was supported by a National Science Foundation grant administered by Harvard University. Barbara Lawrence, Curator of Mammals at Harvard's Museum of Comparative Zoology, was chief investigator for the grant project. She conducted the skeletal and skull examinations of the animals.

It all began about a decade ago near Newport, New Hampshire, a town thirty-five miles northeast of Boscawen. Reports trickled into the Fish and Game Department of a wolflike animal having been spotted by a night snowplow operator. Hunters made similar reports, and Kirk Heath of Enfield made a tape recording of strange howlings he heard in the woods near his home on a still winter night.

Eventually a few deer were killed inside Corbin Park near Newport, a private game preserve, and the wolflike creature was believed to be the culprit. Four of the creatures were tracked inside the park by men on snowshoes. The trackers met no success until one of them noticed fresh dirt on the snow by one of the tracks. The man reasoned that the animal had recently emerged from a den and had shaken the dirt from itself. Backtracking, he found the den. Inside were five pups, not yet weaned.

Three of the pups were females and two were males. They were the nucleus of the Silvers' project. About eighty offspring were born of the original five and their children.

Again and again, as the original five and their offspring were mated, the issue was always "true." That is, there was no substantial difference in the latest-born from the original five, thus destroying the first-popular theory that the animal was a hybrid, a dog-coyote.

Indeed, as the original five reached maturity, the Silvers began to feel sure that they were not dealing with an animal whose parentage involved a domestic dog. The creatures remained unusually shy with strangers, although affectionate with the Silvers.

They demonstrated an unusual climbing ability, and when running on a long leash or in a large kennel they often paced, unlike a dog. They also shed, or molted, most of their heavy fur when warm weather arrived.

(This column was published in November, 1967.)

Lead Poisoning from Spent Shot Threatens North American Ducks

In the days of the old Wild West many desperados who shuffled off this mortal coil were said to have died of "lead poisoning." In that instance, "lead poisoning" meant that a well-directed bullet from a lawman's .44 Colt had done the deed.

Over the years the tons of lead pellets fired at ducks and geese have pattered gently, but not harmlessly, upon shallow inland waters. Diving ducks, including mallards and pintails, when feeding on the bottom unavoidably ingest some of these pellets, which create toxic fluids, and the result is sickness or starvation.

In 1965 the director of the United States Bureau of Sport Fisheries and Wildlife informed Canadian and United States ammunition and firearms manufacturers that waterfowl losses by lead poisoning were becoming too serious to ignore. It was possible, the manufacturers were told, that lead poisoning might make it necessary to shorten hunting seasons or further reduce bag limits.

Apart from its toxic effects on waterfowl, lead is the ideal element for shot. No other metal, with the exception of gold, silver, and certain other precious metals, offers such ideal ballistic characteristics.

Studies by the Illinois Institute of Technology Research Institute, in cooperation with the Bureau of Sport Fisheries and Wildlife and the aforementioned manufacturers, have resulted in the discovery of a supersoft iron that when formed into shot performs similarly to lead ballistically. And the iron shot does not poison waterfowl.

Various other pellets had been tested and found lacking. One process that seemed to have promise was the forming of shot made from lead powder bound together with a water-soluble adhesive so that the pellets would dissolve after being in the water for a short period. Combining lead with other metals, or coating it with plastics, was also tried, but it failed to reduce toxicity.

Early experiments with iron shot were not promising. It was difficult to produce in consistent pellet sizes, and its ballistic performance was poor because of relatively low density. It also eroded gun barrels and deformed chokes. ("Choke," in simplest terms, is a constriction or variation in diameter of a shotgun barrel that tends to keep the charge from spreading too rapidly. Early shotguns had no choke and their effective range was severely limited.)

The supersoft iron shot, which can be formed from wire, will not be commercially available for some time. Its advent will not, of course, immediately do away with waterfowl lead poisoning. Pellets from a century of shooting are already on the bottom, but in many cases silt deposits will make them inaccessible to diving ducks.

Winter

Memories of the Year Just Past Evoke a Bittersweet Pleasure

From the twelve months past I remember a black duck falling down the red west;

Six geese scything a gray sky, far out of range, framed in the branches of a dead white oak;

The moon on the white beach at Andros, black rocks in the water, and their black shadows; rustling palms at my back and behind them the feathery pines;

Quail piping across a damp dawn in Georgia, and the eager pointers ranging;

A black New England night, and stripers in the surf's white water; blue claw crabs, in a flashlight's beam, clinging to the shifting bottom in the outrunning tide from the saltwater pond, and circles drawn in sand by sharp fingers of beach grass;

Laurel leaves and serviceberry blossoms gleaming in the Blue Ridge Mountains and lovely Harper Creek, and the dark shadows of brown trout in its bright waters;

Rafts of bluebills on the Hudson, paddling from shore as the train went past; barges in tow on the broad Tappan Zee, and the ghosts of the river's long-gone sloops running upriver on a fair tide;

The haunting sound of water sliding over miles of tidal flats in

James Bay and the shore birds coming before, blue geese wheeling in the sun, and the swift, erratic flight of snipe at dawn;

Cape Hatteras Light towering through the fog, and the long, rolling surf where bluefish herded frightened mullet across the green miles;

White bluffs of Long Island under the moon in the hour before dawn, and later the tiny skiff wallowing in the seas and filling with bluefish as terns screamed overhead;

Hooked tarpon walking on the water off Flamingo, and the larger ones, the giants that would not hit, rolling ponderously in the brown water;

A snowshoe rabbit drifting like a ghost in the midday twilight of a hemlock swamp, and far behind him the busy beagle's cry;

The red and gold belly of a brook trout shining in the sun as he rolled beneath the fly, gay in the formal dress of procreation, brighter than the bleeding maples or the golden beeches;

Wood smoke creeping from a farmhouse chimney far below, and the smell of wood smoke, which is both promise and farewell, the tree's last fire after flaming through a hundred falls;

Casting for muskellunge under Minnesota's broad skies, and ducks bursting from wild rice along the shore;

Pulpwood logs clogging the Kennebec, and a smallmouth bass shattering the smooth, dark water;

Six does dancing on a Pennsylvania ridge while a blue jay's metallic cry filled the forest;

An old anglerfish dying on the shore at Menemsha, his sagging, leathery skin drying in the sun, huge mouth drinking air convulsively while the hungry herring gulls waited, for the sea wastes nothing.

Vineyarders Face
Foul Weather to Harvest
Succulent Scallops

Edgartown, Massachusetts

A twenty-five-knot wind was screeching out of the north-northwest, and large pellets of cold rain stung our faces as we left Edgartown Harbor on Martha's Vineyard Island for the scalloping grounds two miles away in Cape Pogue Pond.

The seas outside the harbor were running three feet high with an occasional four-footer tossed in for excitement, but Stephen Gentle, Jr.'s, beamy sixteen-foot catboat handled them easily, although there was often five inches of water sloshing about in her self-bailing cockpit.

Some of the boats of the Edgartown scalloping fleet were moving with us toward Cape Pogue Pond, but the skippers of the smaller craft compromised by dragging, or fishing as it is called locally, for scallops near the mouth of the harbor or in sheltered Katama Bay.

The call of scalloping is one that many Vineyarders are unable to ignore, even if they are gainfully employed when fall and the scallop season arrives, and Vineyard employers know that some of their men will always take time off from their regular jobs to pursue the succulent bivalves. If fishing is good, as it has been in Edgartown waters this year, the money is also good, although scalloping is more than that to many islanders. It is also a fever, a way for a man to be his own master, to make a living from the sea even though the work is cold and hard.

Some Vineyard women also go scalloping. It is not unusual to see a wife bundled in oilskins working side by side with her husband, sorting scallops on the boat's culling board. There are even a few mother-son scalloping teams on the island. A two-person team is, of course, allowed to harvest twice the commercial limit, whatever it may be.

Gentle and I left the dock at 7 A.M. and were back before ten with the five bushels of scallops permitted him as a commercial fisherman and the half-bushel allowed me on my family permit. Gentle's five bushels would yield about four gallons of scallop meat, which would bring between eleven and twelve dollars a gallon. Many scallopers pay someone to open their harvest. The usual rate for "cutting" scallops is three dollars a gallon.

Not including the cost of the boat, the average scalloper will spend about one thousand dollars outfitting. Most of this is for the heavy metal dredges that are towed along the bottom behind the boat.

The Vineyarders are pursuing the bay scallop, which ranges from Nova Scotia to Texas in shallow water. (It is, to provide further identification, the almost ubiquitous insignia of the Shell Oil Company service stations.) The other scallop gathered along the Atlantic Coast is a larger, deep-sea scallop, which is dredged from depths as great as one hundred fathoms by oceangoing fishing boats. The bay scallop is considered to be the tastier of the two.

Scallops are among the few mollusks that can swim, and they also have limited powers of sight. The scallop, unlike, say, the quahog or the steamer clam, has a single adductor muscle that holds the two halves of its shell together. It is this large, white, single muscle that is cut out for food, although the stomach and other parts are also good to eat.

Virginia Offers Good Fishing in Salt Water Most of the Year

Virginia Beach, Virginia

The main course of our evening meal at the Princess Anne Inn was baked striped bass, fish we had caught the same day.

The two visiting Yankees, Al Ristori of the Garcia Corporation and I, were content, but the three charming Virginians who had introduced us to the area's winter striped bass angling were chagrined that we had not done better.

In two days of fishing out of Rudee Inlet we caught four bass, all on the second day, averaging about four pounds each. This is not typical of early December striper fishing in the area, but a long stretch of rough, unsettled, and cold weather had taken its toll, and the fish were scattered or not feeding.

Our companions the last day and that evening were Jeff Dane, an executive of WTAR-TV of Norfolk, Virginia, Ray Richardson, a Virginia Beach businessman and charter-boat skipper, and William Thigpen, a wiry little Scotsman who never misses a chance to hunt or fish.

WTAR-TV sponsors the Winternational Striped Bass Derby, which is demonstrating to out-of-state anglers that it is possible to take the prize striper in the Tidewater area of Virginia long after he is no longer available off New England, New York, or New Jersey. The winning fish in last year's derby weighed a respectable fifty-two pounds.

Much of the striper fishing near Virginia Beach involves trolling along the towering concrete legs that support the above-water portions of the Chesapeake Bay Bridge-Tunnel, which was completed more than four years ago and which has proved attractive to stripers and other species.

The first day of fishing, Ristori, Thigpen, and I went out with Wayne McLeskey, a Virginia Beach contractor and real-estate developer, in his Miami 29, a fast and able craft. It was a crisp, sunny day with a strong southwest breeze, but the water was roily and we had no hits.

The second day we went to work in earnest, rising before dawn and setting forth from the inlet in Richardson's thirty-six-foot Richie as red streaked the eastern sky. In the wind and intermittent cold rain that followed, we trolled, in the company of a dozen other boats, the tunnel-bridge complex near West Island in the Baltimore Channel and took our fish, most of them on small bucktails.

The bucktails are fished on the bottom with as much as twenty ounces of lead, although there are many happy occasions when the fish are on the surface and can be taken by casting. Small bass are usually caught along the bridge-tunnel in daylight, and large ones on big plugs and plastic eels at night. Larger fish are also caught in the ocean off Virginia Beach and Cape Henry by daytime trollers.

There are a dozen blue water charter boats and two party boats at the inlet, all members of the Atlantic Charter Service, Rudee Inlet, Virginia Beach, telephone (703) 425-2953. Rudee is the only Virginia Beach boat basin with direct access to the ocean.

January is really the only nonfishing month of the year off Virginia Beach. Atlantic mackerel arrive in great numbers in February and March, big bluefish hit in June, and schools of white marlin are offshore July through September. Hundreds of them were caught by Rudee Inlet boats last summer. The big blues make a second run in the fall, followed by large stripers.

There are also sea trout, spot, Spanish mackerel, flounder, and tautog, and recently great numbers of sea bass have been discovered at the sites of offshore wrecks.

Campfire Meal Dulls Hunger of New Hampshire Deer Hunters

North Charlestown, New Hampshire

As we climbed the steep western flank of Hubbard Mountain, the three young men cast curious eyes at the pack on my back but asked no questions, apparently believing that if an old-timer of forty-six wanted to lug along extra weight, it was his own business.

In that pack were various cooking utensils, tea, coffee, several pounds of good steak, two kinds of dehydrated soup, two small onions, a pound of bacon, and a loaf of rye bread.

There are many ways to hunt deer. One may, for example, work hard at it from dawn to dusk without let-up, perhaps munching a candy bar for quick energy. One may also spend the day at the edge of a meadow a few hundred yards from the starting place.

In earlier years, Victor Pomiecko of Claremont, New Hampshire, and I were in the first category, occasionally meeting at a predetermined spot in the woods for a noon cup of tea. Recently, however, we usually have expanded teatime to full-fledged lunch. One probably hunts better with hunger as a companion, but a good woods-cooked meal is too pleasurable to pass up.

Reaching the top of the mountain, the lads, Roger Adams and Henry Sanders, both of Claremont, and my oldest son, Steve, entered the woods with Vic and me following. Half an hour later Sanders had a difficult running shot at a doe and missed.

We continued to work slowly through the rugged area of mixed hardwoods and hemlocks, covering a patch perhaps two miles long and a mile wide, but we saw no more deer that morning or that day.

Once I moved past three hunters who were shouting directions at each other across a deep ravine thick with hemlocks. One had a chronic cough, and when the wind was still he could be heard for two hundred yards.

I passed unnoticed within fifty feet of the cougher and made no attempt to attract his attention. It is sometimes wise to make one's presence known, particularly if the cover is thick, because a few hunters shoot at movement alone, but there is a certain satisfaction in going undetected and knowing that one is more alert than the other fellow.

If mutual observation does take place, good hunting manners require that one offer no more than a wave of hand. Some hunters greet a stranger with glad cries. This can be disconcerting to a man who has spent hours working silently into the area. If you must talk, move quietly toward your man until you are beside him and speak low. He will respect you for it.

The cougher and his companions will get nothing, I thought, if they continue to slam about the woods in that fashion. Later several shots came from their direction, and at the end of the day we learned that they had taken a small buck. We called it luck. It could not have been anything else.

At noon we met in a clearing high on the mountain and gathered good, dry wood for a cooking fire—dead ash and oak. Vic also discovered a spring hole covered by a flat rock, apparently constructed by the men who had logged the area half a century before. The water was sweet, clear, and cold, the food was good, and far below us in the misty valley, dogs barked and automobiles crept like bugs on the black highway.

All the food was consumed, although Sanders did balk at eating rye bread soaked in bacon drippings. We told him it was excellent cold-weather fodder, but he steadfastly declined.

Visit to a Tavern Brightens End of Dismal Hunting Day

Woodbourne, New York

Once, late in the morning, the ground fog was so dense that I spent twenty minutes stalking a swaying strip of bark hanging from a yellow birch; magnified and distorted, it had resembled the head of a deer.

Later, when the fog had thinned so that it was sometimes possible to see clearly for thirty yards, a bitter, heavy rain streamed down through the trees, and the forest was filled with the sound of water falling on sodden leaves.

Although it had been raining off and on for four days, some snow still remained on the ground and deer tracks were plentiful. The deer were ghostly wraiths: quick brown shapes moving with infinite grace too far ahead for me to see if any had horns three inches or longer, which would have made them legal game.

My companion, Dan Bodner of Napanoch, who is the Sullivan County representative for the public relations and advertising company of Roy Blumenthal International Associates, Inc., fared no better than I.

We slunk dripping from the woods at four o'clock and immediately repaired to the Town and Country Tavern in Woodbourne, where we agreed—after having been inspired by several mugs of tonic, heaping plates of spaghetti and meatballs, and the soft voice and bright smile of Joyce, the prettiest bartender in the county—that it had been a perfectly splendid day.

Viewed objectively, however, Monday, November 18, 1968, will be remembered as one of the least desirable opening days for deer hunting in the Catskills.

Forty or fifty shots were fired in the area we hunted, but we heard of only one buck being killed, and the rumor was that he had missed a sharp turn on the trail at high speed and had run into a tree.

There was a great deal of shouting and blowing of police whistles during the day as separated hunters tried to regroup. The members of one tightly knit band got around this by holding hands as they tiptoed through the thickets, and they were properly incensed when another man, a perfect stranger, tried to join them.

It was all good fun, however, and no one was lost for more than half a day, including one whistle-blower who found himself inadvertently directing traffic on Route 42.

The deer, meanwhile, crept under laurel bushes or hemlock boughs and waited for night to end the foolishness.

Cold Snap and Ice Spoil North Carolina Duck Hunt

Ocracoke Island, North Carolina

A skim of ice twice the thickness of a windowpane held the big skiff and its load of decoys in cold embrace at Quork's Hammock Creek, and our guides, Earle Gaskins and Paul Teeter, were not happy.

Our goal was a sink-box blind a mile offshore in Pamlico Sound, but between us and the blind there was the thin ice in the creek and a half mile of heavier ice, up to an inch thick, broken here and there by open water.

We spent half an hour working through fifty yards of the creek, until Gaskins, who was running the boat for Captain Thurston Gaskill, a long-time Ocracoke charter-boat skipper and waterfowl guide, announced that it was useless to try anymore.

"I sure would like to get you gentlemen out there," he said, "but it would take most of the day and we'd tear the boat to pieces."

The only thing left for Joel Arrington of Raleigh, North Carolina, and me to do was to set up in a shore blind a few hundred yards away. We broke a hole in the ice several yards square in front of the blind and put out a few decoys.

For the remainder of the day we sat in the bright sunlight sipping hot coffee and eating the sandwiches provided us by George Wilkes, proprietor of Ocracoke's Island Inn.

Shore birds and laughing gulls flew past, and warblers teetered on tall stalks of coarse marsh grass in the brisk breeze and perched on top of our blind looking in at us.

Out in the sound, beyond the half mile of ice, small bunches of ducks flew back and forth, and twenty or thirty Canada geese settled down in a patch of open water five hundred yards away, joined later by buffleheads and black ducks. The goose season had already closed and we were hunting the next to the last day of the duck season, but neither ducks nor geese came near us.

To our rear, on the ocean side of Ocracoke Island, large flocks of Canada and snow geese (snow geese are protected all year) flew northeast toward Cape Hatteras throughout the early part of the afternoon. By three o'clock it was clear that we were not going to have any shooting and probably would not have any the following day unless we could reach the offshore blind.

There are public waterfowl shore blinds all along the Cape Hatteras National Seashore, which stretches for more than one hundred miles along the Outer Banks from Whalebone Junction to Ocracoke Inlet. Some are on a first-come, first-served basis, while reservations must be made for others through the office of the seashore's superintendent, whose address is Post Office Box 457, Manteo, North Carolina 27954.

Ocracoke has two other waterfowl guides in addition to Gaskill and his partner Oscar Burrus: Alec Ely, the owner of the Pony Island Motel, and Charles Garrish.

The average cost for a guide and offshore blind is fifty dollars a day for two persons—the number that can shoot from the blind. This does not, of course, include food and lodging.

Waterfowl hunting all along North Carolina's Outer Banks was excellent this year except for the last few days of the season, when bitter cold brought the ice. Black ducks and canvasbacks were in good supply, as were pintails, gadwalls, shovelers, redheads, and brant. Canada goose shooting was fair to good.

Outer Banks Residents
Also Like Salt Pork

A liking for salt pork, whether lean or fat, and salt fish is common among the older residents of seacoast New England. Although their grandchildren seemed to prefer frozen pizzas and TV dinners, it gave me, as a middle-aged New Englander, a twinge of nostalgic pleasure to discover on a recent hunting trip to North Carolina's Outer Banks that salt pork figures prominently in many of the old-time recipes there.

On Ocracoke, the southernmost island of the Outer Banks, a narrow, sandy, lightly forested strip of land seventeen miles long and no more than a mile and a half across at its widest point, the ladies of the Woman's Society of Christian Service of the United Methodist Church sell their Ocracoke Cook Book for one dollar, and many of its recipes call for salt pork.

Take, for example, the instructions for cooking old drum, that is, a large channel bass (many anglers believe the old drum is not worth eating, but the frugal ladies of Ocracoke disagree).

The old drum recipe, attributed to Mrs. Dell Scarborough, follows.

"Put one side of drum, if large, in a large baking pan. Sprinkle salt and pepper on fish; then fry out fat salt pork and pour over all the fish. Sprinkle with chopped or sliced onions. Peel eight potatoes; slice them and put in pan where fish does not cover, then cover fish and potatoes with water. Bake in not-too-hot oven for two hours or until brown. Serve with corn bread and cole slaw. Serves about eight people (if small drum is used, bake whole.)"

So reinforced, you may be sure, a seafaring man could face the treacherous waters of Hatteras and Ocracoke inlets with energy and confidence.

This old drum recipe, I feel rather certain, would work well with a large striped bass, whose meat is somewhat more delicate in flavor and texture than that of the drum.

Two recipes for clam chowders in the Ocracoke Cook Book have a New England ring to them, all beginning with pieces of salt pork fried until brown, and including potatoes and onions. None, however, use milk. (As an aside, try substituting evaporated milk, full strength, for the regular milk called for in a conventional quahog chowder and note the added richness in flavor and texture.)

My fondness for salt pork is excessive. For example, salt pork is always in my knapsack on a camping trip, and my idea of a splendid lunch is fried salt pork with onions and potatoes sliced thin and fried in the fat. If there are a couple of brook trout and a few wild mushrooms to go along with this, so much the better, and cholesterol be damned.

Connecticut Hunters Suffer and Get Limit of Broadbills

Branford, Connecticut

You have to suffer to get good broadbill shooting," said my companion as we sat in the wind and the rain on Sedge Island.

The day was too warm for all-out anguish, although the quality of our suffering improved when the gentle easterly breeze swung into the south and increased to twenty knots, carrying a cold rain in its teeth.

The hunt was a return engagement. A week ago Oliver "Bud" Beckley took me duck hunting and we saw thousands of broadbills but got none. This time I drove away with my three-duck limit.

Beckley is supervisor of game management for the Connecticut Board of Fisheries and Game. From the windows of his Branford home you can look out over Long Island Sound and see the broadbills rafting. When I arrived at his place at noon, he led me to the window and pointed to a dark line of birds bobbing on the water a half mile away.

"They've been sitting there all morning. Whenever the fog lifted, I could see them. If the wind will shift and blow the fog away we should have good shooting."

Beckley is a lover of broadbills. (The broadbill is also called

213

bluebill, and technically is known as a scaup, greater or lesser. Most of the birds on the Sound, which is a major wintering ground for them, are greater scaup.) He doesn't look down on a black duck or a mallard or a teal, but the hardy broadbill claims most of his attention and devotion.

We donned our foul-weather gear, bailed three inches of water out of his skiff, and headed for Sedge Island, one of the numerous rock piles that thrust up from the water off Branford and Guilford.

"I'd like to get an old squaw drake. I have a friend, Grant Briggs, here in Branford, who carves decoys and miniatures and he's working on an old squaw right now. He needs one to get the coloration," Beckley said.

We put out our blocks, about forty-five broadbills and half a dozen black ducks, and retired to the box. We sat with our backs against barnacle boulders and our feet in the tidal wash. The fog closed in until it was difficult to see the outermost decoys, which were about forty yards away.

Lulled by the sound of the gently undulating waves and half mesmerized by the swirling pageant of fog, I was ill-prepared when six old squaws streamed by on my right. They saw our decoys, but obviously had no intention of joining them. By the time I got my gun up only the last in line, a mature drake, was in range. I fired, he nose-dived, and Grant Briggs had his bird.

No broadbills moved for an hour; then the wind shifted, the rain came, whitecaps built up, and small groups of birds began to fly. We picked up our limit, one by one, with some rather sloppy shooting.

"That's the trouble when the birds aren't handling right," Beckley said. "You get overanxious, tighten up, and shoot poorly."

"Handling right" is a catchall phrase Beckley uses, meaning, loosely, that birds aren't coming into the decoys with regularity.

His hooded, grinning, weathered face appeared between two weed-covered boulders on my left, rain and spray streaming off it, eyes shining.

"In a few more days, when the bonus scaup season opens, that's

214

the time. Then you can really suffer and get some good shooting," he said.

My fingers were numb before we got our blocks picked up and back in the baskets, three-foot seas were running, often a cold wave dashed over the windward rail as we raced the darkness home, and behind us on the windswept Sound thousands of hardy broadbills settled down for a night's rest.

While the Surf Roars, Waterfowlers Wait, Shivering, for Bluebills

West Tisbury, Massachusetts

From our blind of hay bales we could see the white line of the surf two miles away, and the sound of it was a never-ending low-pitched roar.

Cold pellets of rain, driven by a stiff northwest wind, stung our faces, and the tall brown grass of the marshes bent before the wind and the rain.

It was the last day of the first half of the Bay State's split season for waterfowl. Behind us in boxes and burlap bags lay fifty bluebill decoys that we had put out before dawn and then picked up in midafternoon when it became apparent that the large rafts of bluebills, or scaup, that were riding out the weather in the center of Tisbury Great Pond were not going to move.

We had taken two stray bluebills and one green-winged teal in the morning, birds that had made a token pass at the bobbing blocks before flaring. Now we were waiting out the last cold hour, hoping the black ducks would be on the move before sunset.

Behind the blind in a cove, an otter cut a furrow across the sheltered water. He was upwind and did not see or smell us. Earlier in the day we had noticed his beaten path up the shore to a knoll under a gnarled white oak. The ground there was marked with his tracks and droppings laden with fish scales.

Buffeted by the wind, a great blue heron flew in from the southeast and landed on the edge of the cove. Balanced on his spindly legs, he turned his head, eyed us, and when one of us moved he lurched aloft, then tumbled downwind.

Later his cousins, the black-crested night herons, or quawks as they are known here, lumbered by, uttering their lugubrious cries. Three wars ago, as a boy hunting these same marshes, I had learned to expect the quawks to precede the black ducks by a few minutes.

And the blacks did come, two of them beating upwind against the torn gray sky on my side of the blind. They were about forty yards away, and when I swung on them I had in my mind that a clean double would be a fine way to end the day. I fired twice, but even before they fell I knew the second shot had gone far behind.

The first charge had got both, and to a casual onlooker it looked as it was supposed to have been. But I knew I was still without my first honest double of the season.

On the way home we discussed the bluebill's reluctance to decoy. There are times when these ducks cannot stay out of a set of blocks, even landing among them when a hunter is picking up downed birds.

The second half of the Massachusetts waterfowl season will undoubtedly bring wild weather and better hunting. It opens December 12 and runs through December 19, with a special bonus black-duck season for certain coastal areas opening December 20 and continuing through January 2 (a special no-cost permit must be obtained from the Fish and Game Department to take blacks during this period).

The Canadian goose season, which closed with the duck season last weekend, also reopens on December 12, but it continues through January 13.

Trained Canada Geese Once Lured Wild Cousins to the Hunters' Guns

West Tisbury, Massachusetts

Forty-nine years ago George Magnuson arrived in this rural hamlet on Martha's Vineyard Island and began an unforgettable apprenticeship in the training of Canada geese as live decoys for hunting.

Young George, then nineteen years old, went to work for Jim Look, a carpenter, commercial fisherman, boat builder, and farmer who also ran a hunting club on the east shore of Tisbury Great Pond. The sixteen club members had exclusive rights to about two miles of pond front property, where they shot ducks and geese all season long.

Magnuson arrived at Look's place in the heart of the gunning season, and he recalls his astonishment at the teams of trained geese that were used to attract their wild brethren within range of the hunters' guns.

"I watched Jim's flyers leave their pens, swing out over the pond, and bring back the wild ones, and wondered how he had trained them," Magnuson said.

In the following eight years, before Jim Look's death, the young man learned how it was done.

Live decoys were banned after Magnuson's first decade on the island, but until that time they were much used by waterfowlers. Live duck decoys were simply staked out or penned on the pond shore, but an elaborate decoying ritual was developed with the more intelligent geese.

What Magnuson saw when he arrived at Jim Look's hunt club was a five-foot-high wooden fence stretching about a half mile along the pond shore. Behind the fence were more than two hundred Canada geese in pens. Twelve pens had ramps leading to the top of the fence. They were for the flyers, the young geese that were sent aloft to bring in the wild ones. Behind the fence and the pens was a clubhouse with a lookout tower, where Jim Look sat and searched the skies for geese.

In the tower was a control panel, with a switch for each flyer pen's electrically released gates.

"Jim would sit there in the tower with his binoculars, looking out over the pond and the ocean," Magnuson recalled. " 'I see some coming in over Long Cove, George,' he would say, and then he would tell me to let one pen go. I would throw the switch, the gate would drop, and the flyers would run up the ramp and launch themselves over the fence. They would fly out to the wild geese and talk to them. 'They're turning! They're turning!' Jim would whisper; then maybe he'd tell me to let another pen go."

If all went well the flyers would bring the geese back toward the fence that concealed the gunners. In front of the fence were the "beach teams," groups of geese staked out at the water's edge. They would also woo the newcomers with their clamorous cries.

Sometimes the flyers brought their unsuspecting cousins over the fence on the wing, and the gunners had to avoid shooting the flyers; each carried a long leather thong on one leg for identification.

At other times the wary wild geese would land on the pond out of range, and the hunters would have to wait to see if the flyers and the beach team could entice them within range.

"Sometimes the wild flock would be one family—goose, gander, and from four to ten goslings," Magnuson said. "The parents would talk to the young ones, warning them that something was wrong, and the flyers and the beach teams would try to convince them otherwise. But if they came in, the hunters would shove their guns through slots in the top of the fence and cut loose. Jim's big Chesapeake retrievers would pile over the fence and retrieve the downed birds."

Maryland Hunt at Remington Farms Successful Despite Poor Shooting

Chestertown, Maryland

We were in our blinds before dawn, shivering in the biting wind, and the moon, no longer an unapproachable mystery, shone cold over the flat corn stubble.

A quarter of a mile before us in Langford Creek we could hear thousands of Canada geese talking incessantly, and we waited impatiently for them and the sun to rise.

To the front and rear of the blinds were dozens of goose decoys, stuffed birds we hoped would attract their live brethren.

By that time those of us who were guests of Remington Arms Company, Inc., at the firm's three-thousand-acre Remington Farms, a farm and wildlife management area on Maryland's eastern shore, had grown accustomed to the sight and sound of large numbers of geese.

Flying in by private plane the previous afternoon, we had seen geese on the Chesapeake Bay ice and on the farm's sanctuary area, and through most of the night the sound of their voices had penetrated the thick walls of the early-eighteenth-century dwelling, the Remington guest house, in which we were bunked.

Rising at six, we had eaten bacon and eggs and sausage prepared by Kelso Smith, the Remington Farms chef, and then had gathered outside to be briefed by the farm's manager, Clark Webster, and his assistant, Hugh Galbreath, both former United States Fish and Wildlife Service biologists.

On our way to the blinds we had been told by our guides and by Edmund S. McCawley, Jr., manager of public relations for Remington Arms, and his right-hand man, Dick Dietz, that the recent cold weather had hurt the hunting, that the geese were not moving about as much as they normally do at this time of year.

But soon after the eight of us who were guests had settled in the pit blinds the action began—so soon, in fact, that one man, Robert Elliot, who is director of vacation travel promotion for the state of Maine, was still fussing with his gear when the first flight came over and fired neither camera nor gun.

The first goose to fall (for those who care, most of us were shooting 12-gauge, high-brass shells loaded with No. 4 shot) set his wings in a long glide that carried him several hundred yards away, but Dan, the farm's Labrador, had watched the bird and soon brought him back.

By nightfall most of us had our daily limit of two geese and two ducks, although a great many shells were fired to achieve that end.

The marksmanship, to put it gently, was spotty, with one possible exception—Hal Steeger of Manhattan. Steeger's credits in our two-day shoot included a single-shot double on two fast-flying mallards. This was only proper, for Steeger is the editorial director of *Argosy,* a magazine for he-men.

A Salute to the Wilderness from One Who Enjoys It

To wild geese calling down the corridors of night,
To girl-slim trout in forest streams, to the flight
Of goldeneyes streaming in from sea at dusk, I drink
A toast. To woodchucks sleeping off summer's fast,
To beavers lolling in their lodges, to the least,
Or lesser, scaup, and the greater, too, to the mink
Who moves like flame across the frozen pond
While the Great Bear trembles overhead and the sound
Of a white oak riven to the heart by bitter cold
Thunders through the white woods, to the bristly band
Of porcupines in their foul den, I extend the hand
Of friendship. To the house of muskrats in the salt
Marsh, to the lissome otter who eats his white perch
Neat, to the fierce shrew whose terrifying search
For food is never done, to the timber wolf, who finds
Divorce anathematic, to the white-tailed deer who digs
Through snow for beechnuts or takes the twigs
And buds of conifers when there is nothing else,
To the partridge whose battering wings beat
Like blood in my ears, to the teal whose fleet,

Erratic flight can make a hunter weep,
To the querulous crow who tumbles across the gray
Sky like an autumn leaf, beloved by few, I say
Happy New Year. To the bobcat who stalks the hemlock
Swamp, and to the snowshoe rabbit he seeks,
To the neurotic red squirrel whose voice squeaks
Like chalk on blackboard through the trees,
To the proud and lonely lynx who cannot learn
To live with man, to osprey and eagle who spurn
Carrion comfort, to catamount and coyote, fox
And mouse, black bear and brown and grizzly, too,
And mountain goat, antelope, heron, green and blue,
To the common tern whose uncommon skill dives
Deeper in my heart than I would care to tell,
To all the songbirds whose bright voices fall
Like stars through my dawn dreams, I give
Deep thanks. To mackerel, striped bass, and blues
Gone south for winter, to tarpon and tautaug, whose
Paths have never crossed, to bluefin tuna
Lurking off the Continental Shelf, to dace
And muskellunge, cod and sculpin, scup and plaice,
To amberjack and alewives, snook and pike,
To all creatures of land and sea and all that fly
I wish a happy '68, keep your birth rates high
And never let a doubt of my best wishes lurk
Within your breasts: without you I am out of work.

Windswept Martha's Vineyard Usually Brown for Christmas

Edgartown, Massachusetts

Early in December, rushing out into the night to greet the season's first snowfall, which was gone in a few hours, my twelve-year-old daughter, Mary, caught several of the large flakes on her tongue and announced that "this year's snowflakes don't taste nearly as good as last year's."

Mary became a connoisseur of snowflakes during the years we lived in New Hampshire—before we returned to Martha's Vineyard Island.

Vineyard children may dream of a white Christmas, but three years out of four it is brown. The water surrounding the island keeps the air temperature several degrees higher than it is a few miles north on the mainland, and what is snow in Boston is usually rain on the Vineyard.

(On December 24 a storm passed out to sea along Cape Cod and the islands of Martha's Vineyard and Nantucket, scarcely touched Boston, and provided islanders with a white Christmas. On December 26, however, another storm, complete with thunder and lightning and torrential rain, washed the islands clean of snow.)

Some Vineyard children circumvent the lack of snow by getting their fathers to tow them along the beach on a flying saucer behind a jeep.

While representing some deprivation for youngsters, the relatively mild winters are welcomed by certain species of wild birds and animals.

For example, no Vineyarder need wait for spring to see his first robin: there are always a few of them that elect to remain deep in some swamp throughout the winter. The Vineyard also has a year-round population of Canada geese and mute swans, and the great blue heron can be found stalking the marshes in January. The bobwhite quail also prospers on the island, helped by the mild winters, ample food and cover, and almost no hunting pressure.

For those who have seen and tasted big snows, and who are not so jaded that they regard snow as a mere inconvenience, there may be a small sadness. Yet there is something haunting and attractive about a brown land, brown scrub oaks, brown grasses and marshlands, and beyond them brown dunes, gray water, and gray sky.

A winter beach is cleansed of superfluities, stark, stripped for elemental conflict with the sea. Gone are the swimmers, the beach umbrellas, the dunnage planks, the mayonnaise, Clorox, wine, and ginger ale bottles tossed overboard from boats; gone are the bits of net, gear, fishing boxes, and odd bits of clothing from both the American and Russian draggers; gone are the striper fishermen; gone are the marvelous little terns that unerringly plucked silvery bait fish from the summer surf.

Along the beach one may see a solitary crow perched on a snag waiting for the sea to bring him supper, or a band of herring gulls squatting on the shore, and there are big eider ducks and tiny dovekies in the surf and bluebills and black ducks in the salt ponds behind the barrier beach.

The beach changes shape during winter storms, and often there is a steep dropoff where an onshore gale and huge waves have hammered for forty-eight hours, and the dunes themselves, held together by deep-reaching roots of beach grass, are flattened, eroded, and sometimes obliterated.

It is a bleak Christmas scene unsoftened by snow or stately spruces, but a scene that somehow makes the lights of home shiny across a dark plain all the more welcome. And where else, one might ask, could the Yule log be a timber from a broken vessel whose copper fastenings burn bright blue?

(This column was published in 1967.)

There Was a Time When This Hunter Wanted to Put Down His Gun

It was the night before Christmas of 1966, and Father came in after dark from goose hunting—too late to have supper with his family, but not too late to say good night to his youngest child, four-year-old Alison.

Ignoring his wet clothes, she wrapped her arms about one of his legs.

"Santa comes tonight," she said, quivering with delight; then descending to more mundane matters, she asked, "Did you catch a goose?"

"No," her father said.

"That's good," she said. "I like geese. I wish you wouldn't shoot things. Why do you? You don't have to. Mummy buys plenty of food at the store."

"I don't know, Allie. I really don't know. Maybe someday I'll stop."

"That would be nice," she responded.

Later, lured into remembrance of things past by fine holiday bourbon and the heat from burning white oak logs in the fireplace, the father thought of a time twenty-two years before when he had resolved never to hunt again.

The snow was deep in the spruces of the Ardennes that late December afternoon in 1944, a fresh snow, a hunter's snow.

The father was one of a company of parachute infantry moving up to the front on foot. The men knew they would be hunting Germans the following day, but the afternoon and evening lay safe before them—they were five miles behind the lines.

Campfires glowed in the semitwilight of the spruces, and around one of the fires the father and four other bearded, helmeted young men relaxed and drank coffee from smoke-blackened canteen cups.

Then the men heard the rapid stutter of a German machine pistol. A whispering went through the tree over their heads and a snow-covered branch, cut by a bullet, fell hissing into their campfire. The company commander and his runner raced by, shouting that a German patrol was in their midst.

The five paratroopers began to hunt. Before they had gone fifty yards they flushed and shot two Germans. The Americans were moving on when one of the fallen soldiers cried out. The man who was later to become Alison's father knelt beside the German. The fatally wounded man plucked a wallet from his pocket and took a picture from it, a picture of a man, a woman, and a child before a small brick house. It was summer and the woman's cotton dress was swirling about her knees.

The German pleaded until the American understood that he was being asked to take the wallet and the picture and to go someday to that small brick house in Germany and tell the woman and the child how their husband-father had died.

"Ja," the American said, nodding his head in affirmative promise. He remained kneeling until the German's breathing ended and darkness came with falling snow among the cathedral trees. As he rose he promised himself that he would never shoot another living thing. He was weary of war, weary of death, and too young to understand the incredible resilience and forgetfulness of the human spirit, its glories and its failures.

Snowshoe Rabbit Is Fast and He Never Holes Up

From the Atlantic to the Pacific in our northernmost states, the snowshoe rabbit holds sway, a compelling challenge to the wintertime hunter.

Smaller than the jack rabbit, larger than the Eastern cottontail, the snowshoe is supremely adapted to the rigorous northern winters.

Equipped with long and powerful hind legs and large feet, the snowshoe can move across deep snow at high speed. Indeed, his speed and ability to jump more than fifteen feet on the flat are all that stand between him and the predators who seek him: bobcats, lynxes, owls, hawks, foxes, coyotes, wolves, and others.

Unlike the cottontail, the snowshoe never lives in a hole or den. His home is a nest, or form, usually under a low-hanging evergreen bough. In this nest the babies are born, eyes open and ready to run.

With the first snows of fall the snowshoe rabbit's pelt begins to change from its summer brown to a protective white that blends into the white of winter. Nature gives him only a partial bleach, however, as the base of the hairs remains brown.

When he has achieved his full winter pelage, only the tips of his ears are dark. Many veteran hunters, especially in failing light, spot him by those ear tips as he moves like a ghost under the trees.

Sometimes the weather plays a cruel trick on the snowshoe rabbit when early snows are followed by thaws and balmy weather. At such a time, particularly if the first snows were on the ground a week or more, the snowshoe is caught in his winter shoe and can be seen for hundreds of feet in the brown woods.

As is the case with many species of birds and animals, the population of the snowshoe rabbit often fluctuates widely. During a peak year in Ontario there were over three thousand snowshoes to the square mile. At the other end of the cycle, however, numbers can drop to one or two animals per square mile.

The snowshoe, also known as the varying hare, can live to five years in the wild and to eight in captivity.

The usual method of hunting snowshoes is with dogs, and beagles are the most widely used. A hunter without a dog can pick up an occasional rabbit if he is adept at spotting them crouching in their forms.

Snowshoes are usually extremely wary, although at times they learn to associate with man. For two years running, there was a snowshoe rabbit who lived on the shores of Lake Solitude atop Mount Sunapee, New Hampshire, who used to come to our campfire in early summer when my sons and I were trout fishing and eat bread and other scraps of food out of our hands.

Because the varying hare is often hunted in deep snow, snowshoes are an essential equipment item. Recommended shot sizes are the subject of contention, as always, but anything from 4's to 7½'s is satisfactory.

Cottontail hunters in quest of the snowshoe rabbit for the first time will find that he moves much faster than his smaller cousin and is always much farther ahead of the dogs. However, the hunter never has to worry about the snowshoe holing up. He will run until he escapes or is shot.

A Good Compass and Topographic Map Necessary Items for a Hunter

During the opening days of the New Hampshire deer season, three northeast storms brought heavy snow to much of the state, and conservation officers were run ragged retrieving lost hunters.

More than seventy-five men were reported lost. Some worked their way out of the woods, some were found by companions, and others were picked up by official search parties.

There is no excuse for getting lost when the sun is visible, but during storms or when there is heavy fog or cloud cover it is easy to get turned around. At such times a compass and a topographic map of the area hunted are important.

The first mistake many hunters make is to rely on road maps, which are not accurate and do not have enough detail.

Neophyte woodsmen should also understand that a compass is of little use unless the man using it knows his general location in the woods.

When setting out, a hunter should know the location of roads, woods roads, trails, streams, swamps, mountains, and valleys for several miles around. He should also know the general direction in which he is moving and he should have a good idea of how much ground he has covered.

If he goes deep in the woods, he should time his hunting so he will be out of the woods at dark while moving at a normal hunting pace. It is foolish to spend the last hour of daylight thrashing at top speed through the underbrush with no chance of seeing a deer when that prime hunting time could have been used to good advantage.

Some men have a highly developed sense of direction, and when it conflicts with what the compass says, a genuine effort of will is required to believe the instrument. Vague doubts enter a man's head at such a time. Perhaps, he reasons, there is a ledge of iron near him that is disturbing the compass, or perhaps the compass itself has unaccountably malfunctioned.

The rule, without exception, is to believe the needle. For assurance, one can always move several hundred yards in the indicated direction and take another reading.

Only once in my life did a compass lead me astray while on land (a ship's compass once went sour, but that is another story). We were climbing Mount Sunapee in Newbury, New Hampshire, in rain and fog, and moisture got into the compass, a cheap version of the U.S. Army lensatic.

We missed a key trail in the fog, went over the mountain and down the other side with full packs, coming but eight miles from where we started and five miles from our goal, a mountaintop trout lake.

This was inexcusable. There are many good moistureproof compasses available for less than ten dollars, and they will last a lifetime, surely a small investment against, at the very least, irritating inconvenience.

Boy's First Day
on the Marshes
Creates Serene Duck Hunter

Huddled in a flimsy duck blind on the shore of a New England salt pond several days ago with rain driven by a sharp southwest breeze stinging my face, I was suddenly and inexplicably amused that I had chosen to spend so many gray November afternoons in a similar fashion, when, with few exceptions, a warm room, a cheerful fireplace, good books, and good conversation had been close by.

It had all begun thirty-five years before, when an eleven-year-old boy with his first shotgun went to the same pond. The Christmas Day was warm, there was wind, and the sun was high and bright. The boy walked to a muskrat house in the marsh, a rounded dome of reeds and grasses. He walked quietly, and a sleeping otter basking in the sun on the opposite side of the muskrat house did not hear his approach.

The boy looked at the sleek, dark, beautiful otter, knowing that its pelt would be worth twenty-five or thirty dollars, wondering whether to shoot it, then reached out with the muzzle of his gun and touched the animal, which after a look of wild surprise, plunged into the water.

Sitting on the muskrat house, enjoying the indescribably rich odor of the marsh, the boy looked south toward the ocean three miles away, and in less than ten minutes a lone black duck flew directly over him, perhaps fifty yards up. The boy fired and the duck fell almost at his feet, landing on its back in the black mud, its red legs paddling feebly in the air.

The boy left, walking home across a meadow grown over with bayberry, blueberry, and blackberry bushes. Having taken his first duck with his first shot was good, but having touched an animal as shy and wary as an otter was an experience that had to be shared as soon as possible.

In the years since that first duck fell, there have been countless other days of duck hunting, some in which a full bag limit was taken, many more in which few or no ducks fell. Always, however, the number of birds downed has been the least memorable part of the day.

This admission places me in the "Serene Duck Hunter" class, first described by President Grover Cleveland in his little-known book *Fishing and Shooting Sketches,* which was published in 1906, nearly a decade after his second term was completed.

To be a Serene Duck Hunter, is to be one who gathers as much enjoyment from the companionship and conversation of other hunters, from the paraphernalia of the hunt, the decoys, the guns, the ammunition, the lore, the literature, as he does from killing birds.

President Cleveland did not mention one important trait of his ideal duck hunter, however: his delight in cooking the few birds he does shoot. To prepare and cook a wild duck supper properly is to have mastered the final step in becoming a Serene Waterfowler.

Vermont Colonel's Sauce Is Good for Rabbits As Well As Birds

Norwich, Vermont

The colonel's sauce triggered the hunt. It was served on blue goose from Canada and woodcock from Vermont, both species shot by Hanson Carroll of Norwich, a free-lance photographer, outdoorsman, and lover of good food.

Hans and I sipped bourbon and waited for his wife, Gloria, to take the goose and the woodcock from the oven. Meanwhile she prepared the colonel's sauce, stepping with practiced skill over her own Chesapeake pup and the children's pet duck, who wandered through the kitchen.

It was a fine sauce, a true game bird sauce, with just the right amount of astringency and sweetness. After tasting it on the birds, I wondered how it would be on snowshoe rabbit.

"We have no snowshoes in the freezer," Hans said, "but we do have Judy."

"If you do hunt Judy, for heaven's sake make a kill in front of her," said Gloria, who is no stranger to rod and gun.

We went to the kennels to look at Judy, an eight-month-old beagle, who was sharing quarters with a big pointer and an adult Chesapeake.

"Does she hunt?" I asked.

"She's run a little. A friend and I just bought her. We've never killed a rabbit with her. A few weeks ago we wanted to go rabbit hunting but couldn't find a dog to borrow, so we paid forty dollars for her."

It should be understood that the borrowing Hans had reference to was with the owner's permission. A frequent gambit in this part of the country for those without access to a dog is to drive around town until a likely beagle strolls by, invite him into the car, hunt him for a day, and return him to the point of embarkation.

It was near zero when we set out with Judy, but that day the cold wave ebbed away from the Northeast, and by noon we were sweating as we worked through the woods on snowshoes.

Judy had not yet learned to use her voice, and she sometimes pottered aimlessly; but she did plow through the deep snow with commendable energy, working out the signs that lay before her.

Because she did not give tongue, we strove to keep pace with her by sight and intuition, always trying to coast ourselves strategically along the rabbit runs.

I have a serviceable excuse for missing my first and only shot. Every shotgunner knows that footwork is one of the keys to success, but when one is wearing snowshoes, footwork is limited. You have to guess whence the rabbit is coming and commit yourself.

I guessed wrong and tried to get off a shot by twisting around. I plucked a little fur from the hare as he sailed silent and ghostlike through the pines, and five minutes later he fell to Hans' 20-gauge —on the second shot, I might add.

When Judy reached the fallen hare, we fed its heart and liver to her and took her home to give her a chance to assimilate her experience, to comprehend that she had finally reached the unseen creatures she had been vainly pursuing for two weeks.

Hans pressure-cooked the rabbit for twenty minutes and commandeered the remainder of the colonel's sauce. We found that it was also a sauce for wild rabbits, and gave thanks to the colonel, who, I was told, was a Vermonter.

The recipe: melt a tablespoon of butter in a frying pan; blend in a tablespoon of flour, a tablespoon of mustard, ¾ cup of orange marmalade, ½ teaspoon grated orange rind, and at least one cup of dry red wine.

Snowshoeing
a Neglected Sport
Entire Family Can Enjoy

Snowshoeing is a sorely neglected sport. People who brave summer's heat, black flies, deer flies, gnats, and mosquitoes to hike woodland trails regard those same trails with hostility when they are deep in snow.

Thus the use of snowshoes, an invention of the American Indian, is limited mostly to bobcat hunters, trappers, timber cruisers, and other men whose occupations call them into the woods in winter.

Skis can be used to tour the snow-filled forest, but most skiers are gregarious souls or are genuinely interested in the speed and challenge of that exacting sport.

Snowshoeing is ideally suited to the person who enjoys solitude and has never had the time or inclination to learn how to ski.

Family snowshoeing parties are a delightful way to spend a winter's day. A campfire, for warmth or cooking, can be built with no danger to the woods. Small children can be towed behind on a toboggan, and there is no better time to introduce them to the pleasures of deciphering animal signs left on the snow.

Basic snowshoe styles are trail, bear paw, and pickerel. The trail shoe is very long and narrow with an upswept toe and is designed for use on deep snow in open country. The bear paw is nearly round and flat and is intended for traveling in dense woods. The pickerel is a shorter version of the trail shoe.

One of the best for general use is a modified trail shoe sold by L. L. Bean of Freeport, Maine. Regular Alaskan trail shoes aren't really needed by the casual user, and the bear paw can drive a neophyte to distraction if the snow is fluffy and deep.

It takes only a few minutes to learn how to use snowshoes, although one shouldn't, unless he's an athlete, try for more than two miles the first time out.

The snowshoer's gait is shambling, but it doesn't have to be spraddle-legged. As you walk, the top of one snowshoe actually rides a few inches above the other and clears it when the stride ends.

Ski poles are helpful when climbing with snowshoes. Without them it is necessary to crab up steep inclines.

When possible, keep your snowshoes outside or in a cold place if you are planning to use them the next day. If they are warm when you start, snow will stick to them, making each step an ordeal.

Bindings are a matter of individual preference, but all good bindings hold the toe of your foot firmly on the snowshoes and allow the heel to ride up and down. Any good outdoor boot can be worn with snowshoes, and many people get by with ordinary overshoes over street shoes.

The cost is not great: you should be able to buy a good pair of snowshoes with bindings for about thirty dollars.

Ice Fishermen Find Ice Auger Superior to an Old Crowbar

Unity, New Hampshire

The pungent bittersweet wood smoke from our cooking fire drifted across Crescent Lake to where we were busily drilling holes through two feet of hard black ice.

It was the first time two of us, Victor Pomiecko of Claremont, New Hampshire, and I, had ever used anything as modern as an ice auger. For years our ice-cutting tool was an old crowbar sharpened to a pencil point, which exploded, rather than cut, the ice. Later Vic fashioned an ice chisel, which proved slightly more effective than the crowbar.

The hand-powered auger, which belonged to Joseph Nawojczyk, also of Claremont, was faster than both and made a neater hole. (For fishermen who dislike the labor involved in cutting ice, there are gasoline-powered ice augers available, and some of them also have an attachment for digging post holes.)

Joe and his twelve-year-old son, Joe, Jr., had already set out several tip-ups, devices that signal when a fish has taken the bait, in this case live minnows. The senior Nawojczyk is an accomplished woodsman, and his son, a pleasant, seemingly imperturbable lad, is already familiar with many of the secrets of field and stream.

Our goal was the chain pickerel, and we soon had several of

them, two weighing more than two pounds each, flopping on the snow-covered ice.

Ice fishing is not for the man who wants dramatic action. Much of it, once the bait is in the water, is waiting, although there are times when the tip-ups signal with pleasing regularity.

The most expensive tip-ups, and the best, are those that have their running gear, the spool of line, under water. Even if the hole ices over, these rigs continue to function. On a relatively warm day this is no problem, but when it is really cold the ice must be skimmed from the holes every few minutes if underwater devices are not used.

Pickerel swim off with a minnow before stopping to swallow their prey, and some provision must be made for the fish to run freely with the line. A century ago men simply tied one end of the line to a piece of brush and left loose coils on the snow or ice. When the branch danced up and down, they knew a fish was on the hook.

Because there are long waiting periods in the cold, a fire, when conditions permit, is welcome. Food and drink may be prepared over it also.

On bitterly cold days bottled warmth provides a welcome diversion, although any quantity of hard liquor and subzero weather are a dangerous combination.

Ten years ago Vic and I snowshoed to a remote mountain pond when the temperature was fifteen below zero and the wind was gusting thirty knots or more from the northwest. We cut our holes, built a shelter with a tarp, and when it came time to sample our wine jug we found it full of frozen slush that would not pour.

Faced with that crisis, we gathered up our gear and fled the howling, inhospitable mountain.

Florida Mosquito Ditches Yield Some Dancing Fly Rod Tarpon

Jensen Beach, Florida

When the wind blew us off the broad reaches of the Indian River, Elwood "Cap" Colvin of Seaside Park, New Jersey, had a suggestion.

"Let's try for tarpon in the mosquito ditches," he said.

The ditches he referred to cut through the swampy ground on the inshore edge of Hutchinson Island, a long, narrow, unspoiled strip of land that can be reached by two causeways in the Stuart-Jensen Beach area.

"The tarpon are landlocked," Colvin said. "Salt water is pumped daily into the ditches through big pipes to keep the mosquitos from breeding. Apparently young tarpon were pumped in with the water along with other bait fish such as mullet. Whatever happened, there are plenty of tarpon in those ditches, snook and mullet. I even heard of a big channel bass being caught in there."

We tried for the tarpon with fly rods, offering them streamers and popping plugs, casting into the slowly moving water at the foot of tightly laced mangrove roots that lined the shores.

As we moved along, herons lunged out of the water ahead of us with raucous shouts of indignation, ducks scuttled off to the side into the deeper recesses of the swamp or went aloft with a roar of wings, and gulls and pelicans flew overhead. Raccoon tracks were everywhere on the shore.

We fished for an hour, until dusk, with no success, although I did get one strike from a tarpon on a popping plug.

"Not many of them around today," Colvin said. "When they are about you can see them rolling."

I returned the following morning and in an hour hooked five tarpon, losing three of them. All were from three to ten pounds and all leaped and thrashed in a silvery dance down the narrow ditch. Sailfish, tarpon, sea trout, bluefish, pompano, whiting, drum, snook, and dozens of other species are available to anglers in this area, and they may be caught in a variety of ways.

Day and night, bridges are lined with fishermen: men, women, children, grandmothers, grandfathers. Gear ranges from light spinning rods to heavy surf rods or long, thick cane poles.

Some of the bridges have special walkways for fishermen below the automobile level. Many anglers bring camp chairs and picnic jugs and baskets and make a day or night of it.

For those who want to become waterborne, there are marinas where craft ranging from the $100-a-day sailfish charter boats to the simple skiff without outboard at a few dollars a day may be engaged. And if you arrive without the proper gear, bait and tackle shops dot the waterfront.

The area is geared to the fisherman. Each evening Stuart's radio station, WTSU-WMCF, tells where fish are being caught and makes predictions for the following day, and every bait shop or marina is a clearing ground for fishing information.

And if a man wants solitude he can find it along the surf-thrown haze of Hutchinson Island's offshore beach, where blues, pompano, whiting, and jack crevalle are currently running.

The Stuart-Jensen area has another attraction for the tourist angler: hotel and motel rates are considerably less than they are to the south along Florida's famed Gold Coast.

Expert Calls Florida a Paradise for Saltwater Fly-Fisherman

Jensen Beach, Florida

"Florida is a saltwater fly-fisherman's paradise," said Elwood "Cap" Colvin as we steamed up the Indian River at 4 P.M. in quest of spotted weakfish, or trout as they are called here.

Colvin should know what he is talking about, for he has been an annual visitor to this community, which is just across the St. Lucie River from Stuart, for fifteen years. He also is the founder of the Saltwater Fly Rodders of America.

With us was Matt Maurer, a retired furniture manufacturer and dealer. Both men live in Seaside Park, New Jersey, where Colvin owns a tackle shop.

A few miles up the river Colvin cut the engine. We were about two hundred feet offshore in three feet of water. The bottom was covered with aquatic vegetation that left only an occasional patch of clear sand.

Colvin and the guest angler worked with fly rods using bright bucktails, mostly yellow and white. Maurer, with a light spinning rod, was offering the fish a small floating plug designed to look like a mullet.

"This is the place for the boozers [big trout]," Maurer said, and on his sixth cast he hooked a two-pounder, the first of five keepers that afternoon. The fish lashed about on the surface for a moment, and then bored down into the grass, twisting and rolling before he was netted.

"See what they do? That's why we use a shocker," Maurer said. The "shocker" was eighteen inches of twenty-five-pound-test monofilaments tied on the end of his ten-pound-test line. This heavy material resists abrasions that would part the lighter line.

We caught ladyfish, slim, silvery, lovely things, which we released. We caught a few small jack crevalle, a handsome, hard-fighting dandy that grossed twenty pounds, and released them. We caught lizardfish, ugly, toothy fellows that resemble an emaciated pickerel.

"Trash fish," Colvin said. "We've got a project. We kill every one we catch."

Fast to another ladyfish, Colvin said, "This is what I was talking about. Up north you can sling a fly all day in salt water without getting a strike. Down here, there's always something."

The wind picked up, pushing us down the river.

On the shore, palm leaves swayed, and between us and the shore several mullet flashed in and out of the water striving to escape some larger fish.

We drifted by two men wearing waders. They were one hundred yards offshore fishing for trout.

Each was fast to a fish as we drew abreast.

A lumbering pelican flew up the river, folded his wings, and crashed into the water after bait fish.

Maurer caught and released three small trout, about fourteen inches long. "We'd better move in, Cap," he said. "The big ones seem to prefer the shallow water."

We boated one more trout before we headed downstream in the gathering darkness, skirting the long gill nets of commercial fishermen, which were marked by lighted buoys at each end.

Brittany Spaniels Help Make Georgia Quail Hunt a Success

Pine Mountain, Georgia

Fortified with a seven o'clock breakfast of grits, fried eggs, sausage, ham, buttered rolls, coffee, and juice and an equally generous portion of Georgia hospitality, Bill Howland and I hied to the Callaway Gardens Hunting Preserve clubhouse to begin a second half-day of quail hunting.

The morning was cool, in the high 50's, and a gentle breeze started up out of the southwest. At the clubhouse we were met by Dutch Martin, the manager of the preserve, and our guide, Ken Sivell.

The previous afternoon we had shot over three setters. This morning we were given a change of pace: two eager Brittany spaniels, Babe and Rex. In ten minutes they were on point at the edge of a small plot of grain that had been planted as forage for the birds.

We moved to within two feet of the bird, a hen, that crouched in the grass inches from one dog's nose. The bird flushed to Howland's right and he made a clean kill about twenty yards out.

"That's the way to start," Sivell said. "Hunt on, Babe. Hunt on, Rex."

For some reason—perhaps it was the steadying influence of the grits—we both shot better that morning, averaging two birds every three shots. A few of the quail were not hit squarely, but none escaped the dogs.

Obeying Sivell's rare and soft-spoken commands to "hunt on" or "hunt close," the merry dogs, their stubby tails ever wagging, found birds with pleasing regularity.

When closing in on a quail they sagged lower and lower until their bellies were almost touching the ground. They were perhaps not as flashy as the setters had been, but they were hard workers and nearly flawless.

Once on the edge of a small stand of pine, we found a pile of quail feathers. Sivell poked at them with his boot. "A hawk did that. See, he left the gizzard. They'll eat everything but the feathers and the gizzard," he said.

Foxes and bobcats also find the Callaway quail good eating, Sivell said.

Almost all the quail on the preserve are reared birds. Martin buys most of them in Alabama and Georgia. Five years ago six thousand quail were bought and released. Last season the figure was 21,150. The hunting season on Georgia preserves runs from October 1 to March 31.

"We should get an 80 per cent return on released birds," Martin said. "Our figure last season was 76.2 per cent."

Hunting at Callaway is thirty dollars a day for a ten-bird limit. Each additional bird costs three dollars.

As eleven thirty drew near, Howland had ten birds and I had nine. He had to leave for Atlanta, eighty-five miles north, at noon.

"The next bird is yours," he said as we worked our way back toward the pickup truck that had taken us out there.

We had already marked the next bird, one I had missed on a crossing shot a few minutes before.

This time the bird, a fat cock, flew straight away, an easy shot, and the ritual was completed.

Spearing Eels through the Ice Is Not a Difficult Task

During the last month eels, beheaded and skinned, appeared in the fresh fish departments of some seacoast New England supermarkets, averaging about seventy cents a pound.

A few of them may have been caught in the fall in traps and kept alive in floating containers, or eel cars, as they are called, but most were taken through the ice by spear fishermen.

Spearing eels through the ice, or from a boat in winter when there is no ice, is not too difficult. The creatures are resting somnolent under the mud or hanging just above the mud in thick concentrations of eel grass and therefore are oblivious to the spear and the fisherman.

The multitined spear does not impale the eels. They are forced between the tines on the downward thrust and held there as the spear is drawn to the surface. A quick upward snap and rapid withdrawal of the spear from the water are essential after an eel is struck or he will squirm free. A handle twelve or fifteen feet long is usual for an eel spear. The water is not often that deep, but the long handle enables one to probe a wide area around a single hole when fishing through the ice.

Here and there in New England one may find manufactured eel spears for sale, and local blacksmiths also turn out a few every fall. In Edgartown, Massachusetts, on Martha's Vineyard Island, Milton Jeffers fashions spears for two dollars a tine. A four- or six-tined spear is large enough for men of average strength and endurance.

Each year young American eels begin their incredible one-year journey from the Sargasso Sea, southeast of Bermuda, where they were born, to the rivers and streams of the Atlantic and Gulf coasts. At the same time their closely related European counterparts leave the same area and start a three-year trip to Europe.

Once along the coast, the eels push upstream until they find fresh or brackish water and remain there from five to twenty-five years until the females are sexually mature. The two sexes then join forces, return to the Sargasso, spawn, and die.

In addition to being prized as food by many people (simple frying is a common way to cook them), eels are devoured in great numbers by such game fish as the bluefish and the striped bass and are frequently used by anglers as bait.

Eels blocked from returning to the sea or their wintering grounds will travel overland. A friend and I learned this the hard way nearly twenty-five years ago. We had several hundred pounds of eels blocked off in a brook. Above the pool they were in was an impassable waterfall and at its lower end was a concrete dam with a fine mesh screen.

In the fall we put all the eels we had caught into the pool, planning to sell them in early winter. Arriving at the pool one November morning we found a slimy trail leading through the grass and over the corner of the dam. Every one of our captives had gone downstream.

Stymied by Weather, Anglers Probe Lair of Weeki Wachee Maidens

Brooksville, Florida

There are times when fishermen must bow gracefully to inclement weather and seek other forms of amusement.

For two days a strong, cold wind and intermittent rain kept John Wilhelm and Fred Archibald, Jr., both of St. Petersburg, Florida, and me from any serious angling for largemouth bass.

Wilhelm and Archibald, who run the Florida Outdoorsman Program for the state's Department of Commerce, have learned to be resourceful, however. Transforming ourselves into tourists, we visited the "Spring of 10,000 Fish" at Homosassa Springs and watched, from a submerged, glass-sided structure, huge snook, jack crevalle, mullet, shad, and catfish milling about. We rode in the deep-draft underwater-viewing tour boats in nearby Rainbow Springs in Dunnellon, and saw big largemouth bass swimming lazily by in the air-clear water.

We journeyed to the shores of Weeki Wachee just in time to observe lissome young women disporting in a clear pool that appeared to be about one hundred feet deep.

These daily "mermaid" shows viewed from beneath the surface

251

of the water through heavy plate-glass windows are well done and fun to see.

David Lagrua, a marine patrol officer of the Florida Department of Natural Resources, introduced us to Ron Bishop, an enthusiastic young executive of the Mid-Florida Aluminum Corporation of Orlando, manufacturers of an air boat, the Air-Gator. Air boats have been around Florida and the Everglades for a long time, but most have been homemade. Bishop's firm is diving headlong into the recreation market. The Air-Gator, driven by an aircraft propeller, travels on water, snow, ice, mud flats, or even wet grass.

With Bishop at the helm, we launched the Air-Gator several miles downstream from the Mermaid Pool in the Weeki Wachee River and ran upstream, seeing ospreys, bald eagles, purple gallinules, limpkins, and alligators.

Arriving at the pool, Archibald and I found another show going on. The management did not respond to our gentle hints that we join the girls in the pool, so we obtained permission to probe their underwater lair after the performance ended.

We visited the underwater mock-up of a spaceship, which has an air chamber inside it, peeked into the tunnel through which the girls enter the pool, then turned and swam downstream for a mile and a half past large schools of silvery ladyfish and shad, past largemouth bass, past shoals of bream, and past an occasional alligator wallow.

Bishop took us aboard on the downstream end of the trip and we learned how tough and stable the Air-Gator is when we slammed into a log slanting down into the stream from shore: she heeled and took water, and there was a slight dent in her bow, but that was all.

The firm, Bishop said, is currently developing a small air boat that will cost about fifteen hundred dollars. This boat, he says, will do everything a snowmobile can do and will also ride on water.

Tiny Florida Keys Deer
Have Big Man for a Friend

Big Pine Key, Florida

Here on one of the outermost Florida Keys lives a big man who has protected America's smallest deer since 1946.

He is Jack Watson of the United States Fish and Wildlife Service, whose domain includes three national refuges extending about seventy miles over scattered keys, or islands: the west to a point beyond East Bahia Honda Key in the east. The refuges are the Key West National Wildlife Reserve (established in 1908), the Great White Heron National Wildlife Refuge (1938), and the National Key Deer Refuge (begun in 1954).

The little Key deer is a subspecies of the Virginia white-tail. Bucks average sixty to ninety-five pounds, does thirty-five to sixty-five. A really large male will stand twenty-nine inches high and weigh about 110 pounds.

By 1947 hunters had reduced the Key deer population to fewer than fifty, even though a law making it illegal to kill the animals had been in effect since 1939. (It is now illegal to hunt anywhere in the Florida Keys.)

Today Watson, who manages the deer refuge, estimates there are about 450 of the animals scattered over several islands. "They're doing fine," he said. "All they needed was a little protection."

Watson has a goal. He believes the refuge could easily support twelve hundred deer. "There's plenty of food, cover, and water. They browse and bed in a narrow band along the shores of the islands. One of their principal foods is the leaves and bark of the red mangrove, and there is so much of it that you have to look close to see any signs of their feeding. That mangrove has a high food value, equivalent to alfalfa. Also, its acid content may have something to do with the deer having no stomach worms and few parasites."

Automobiles take their toll of the deer. Twenty-five were killed in that manner in 1967.

Beginning in 1946, Watson was able to give the deer some protection. Part of their habitat fell within his own province, the heron refuge. Later, private organizations and foundations helped pay for the additional cost of protecting the deer and provided funds to acquire acreage for the deer refuge in addition to that bought with the $35,000 Congress appropriated in 1957.

Watson, who is a large and seemingly tireless man, wages a never-ending battle against poachers. Much of his work is done at night, when he prowls Big Pine and Little Torch Keys in his car.

"I never go out at the same time. That keeps them on edge. Also, I know who they are. There are half a dozen from Key West, a few boys from Marathon (a nearby Key), and a few more from the west coast of Florida. Times have changed since I began. People help me now. Many times I get tipped off that someone is going to try some poaching."

Watson also gets reports from fishermen and from a patrol plane that flies over the area twice a week. He patrols in an outboard cruiser that has a top speed of thirty-five miles an hour.

About 150,000 people visited the refuge in 1967. Many of them came to see the two deer, a buck and a doe, that are kept in large pens near Watson's headquarters.

The male, now five years old, was patched together after he was hit by a car when he was eleven months old. The female was rescued while drowning off one of the keys. Watson nursed her through several bouts of pneumonia.

(This column was published in February, 1968.)

Shipwrecked Anglers Spend Night on Florida's Remote Cape Sable

Flamingo, Florida

We were cruising along the lovely, lonely shell-strewn beaches of Cape Sable, the southernmost portion of the United States mainland, when the big outboard on Vic Dunaway's twenty-foot Sea Craft made dismal sounds and died.

Dunaway, former outdoor editor of the Miami *Herald,* Bernard "Lefty" Kreh, outdoor writer and director of the Metropolitan Miami Fishing Tournament, and I soon discovered that the motor's ills were beyond simple emergency repairs.

We dropped anchor a half mile offshore, halfway between Middle Cape and Northwest Cape, and for lack of anything better to do, we began to fish. The time was 10:30 A.M. We caught a few sea trout, several small sharks, catfish, a houndfish, and a small member of the skate family while keeping watch for a boat to hail.

In early afternoon a good-sized sloop went by us in the Gulf of Mexico, beating up against the strong northwest wind, but she was a mile or more away and apparently did not see us waving our orange foul-weather gear.

At three thirty we rigged a makeshift sail from two rain jackets, using a heavy boat rod for a mast, and headed for shore. The wind was blowing at a slight angle off the shore, so the question was whether we could hit Northwest Cape before we went past it out into the Gulf. In an hour's sail we moved three miles laterally along the beach and came abreast of the cape about one hundred yards offshore. From there we edged the boat to the beach by repeatedly tossing the anchor overboard and pulling up to it.

In another hour we had a good driftwood fire going, made beds with boat cushions, and took stock of our provisions, which included soft drinks and water, crackers, cookies, sardines, cans of corned beef and deviled ham and Vienna sausage, a thermos of coffee, and two of the sea trout we had caught. We split the trout, fastened them to a piece of plywood with leader wire, and broiled them next to the fire.

Kreh gave me a lesson in his unusual fly-casting technique. Without a double haul he can throw a fly one hundred feet with ease. While we were doing this a light plane came out of the sunset. We waved our jackets, the pilot changed course, circled us once, waggled the plane's wings, and flew on.

After sunset, roving bands of hungry mosquitoes came out of the grass and feasted on us. We donned our foul-weather gear, anointed ourselves with insect repellent, and settled down for the night.

It was my impression that the mosquitoes found me more palatable than my companions, and being unable to sleep except for short intervals, I kept myself amused by feeding the fire.

The night was calm and the waters of the Gulf smooth. Stars gleamed in the clear sky, an occasional jet plane passed by high overhead, and in the early morning a young moon, with the old moon in its arms, rose behind a sable palm.

Shortly after sunrise Carl M. Fleming, an Everglades National Park ranger from the Flamingo station, arrived in his launch. The pilot of the plane, whose name was not available, had reported us to Marathon on the Florida Keys and Marathon had relayed the message to Flamingo.

Small Tarpon Off Flamingo Prove Difficult to Land

Flamingo, Florida

After hooking and losing five tarpon in as many casts, I was able to persuade a twelve-pounder to remain on the line.

The others had flung the plug back to me on the first or second leap, but after the sixth fish had burst from the water three times, the skipper of the twenty-seven-foot charter boat *Comorant,* John Allen, a transplanted Tennessean, remarked laconically, "I guess you've got him. If you keep him through three jumps you usually do."

In another five minutes the fish was alongside the boat and released.

It was then that one member of a boatload of life-jacketed people in a skiff sixty yards away yelled: "What was that?"

"Tarpon," Allen shouted back, then mumbled something under his breath.

The occupants of the skiff resumed their fishing. They were out for food, bait-fishing on the bottom for such tasty panfish as mangrove snappers. (Tarpon, for those who don't know it, are not worth eating.)

Tarpon ranging from five to twenty-five pounds were rolling and finning all about us and we took a few more, but the skiff anglers stuck to their food-fishing. And that epitomizes the angling at Flamingo. There is room for everyone, for the camper who wants to catch his evening meal and for the man who wants to specialize in a certain game fish.

Flamingo is within the Everglades National Park, as is most of Florida Bay, the waters that wash its shores.

Campsites for everything from tents to housetrailers are available at Flamingo and at another point near the park's entrance, thirty-eight miles north.

Flamingo is ideally suited for a family trip, or for the man who likes to fish and the wife who doesn't. If she is a bird-watcher, the husband can safely spend long hours on the water without fear of recrimination, for the park abounds in bird life: pelicans, brown and white; gulls, terns, skimmers, roseate spoonbills, herons, coot, pintail ducks, mallards, purple gallinules, bald eagles, snowy egrets (whose feathers were once sold for thirty-six dollars an ounce), and cattle egrets, to name a few.

There are also otters, deer, alligators, crocodiles, opposums, and raccoons within the park.

There are slide lectures every night by park rangers and tours and boat rides in all directions during the day. If you don't like guided tours, you can see most of the places on your own. One of the unusual boat rides is to Cape Sable, where those who fancy exotic seashells can find them in profusion on the surf-washed beach, the southernmost extremity of the United States mainland.

Massive Tarpon Showers Angler As He Leaps beside the Boat

Flamingo, Florida

Those who have seen a massive, gleaming tarpon hurtle out of the water in a shower of spray, shaking his great head in an effort to rid himself of the hook, are almost as much captured as captor.

Thus it was that Ken Wilkey, general manager of the Flamingo Lodge, cottages, and marina, stood shaken in the stern of the boat, dripping with the water a tarpon estimated to weigh seventy-five pounds had flung over him from eight feet. In his first marvelous leap the fish had also broken free. Wilkey stared silent and enraptured at the place where the fish had appeared.

"Oh, my! Oh, my!" exclaimed our skipper, John Singleton. "Wasn't that beautiful? And it's just as beautiful when you've seen it a thousand times."

Wilkey's fish hit late in the afternoon, our first tarpon of the day. Before that we had toured Whitewater Bay and adjoining bays and rivers in the Everglades National Park, stopping occasionally to drift and cast.

Three days before, a great school of tarpon had been feeding in the bay for a week, but a cold northerly wind had put them down. Our day was the first of a warming trend, which later proved to be short-lived, and Singleton spoke to the sun: "Come on, sun. Shine down. Those tarpon haven't left; I know they haven't. All we need is a good warm sun."

As if in answer to his pleadings, the sun seemed to gain strength as the hours wore on; the breeze slacked off and patches of heavy clouds began to disperse.

We cruised for miles looking for tarpon leaping or for the bubbles they produce after coming up to breathe. For the most part we fished "blind" for them, throwing our lures where there were no such signs. We caught sea trout, mangrove snappers, and jack crevalle, but no tarpon.

Then, at three thirty, a few rolled as we drifted in a long eddy off a mangrove island. It was there that Wilkey got his first strike, on a deep-swimming, red-headed Mirrolure. He quickly lost two more tarpon, both fifty pounds or better.

"They're hitting right on the bottom," Wilkey said, and a search through my tackle box produced a deep-running muskellunge plug called the Cisco Kid, last used in Cass Lake in Minnesota. On the sixth cast with it, a good fish hit and I hit back. He thundered out of water, gill plates opened wide, perhaps a forty-five-pounder. Then the line broke. He jumped several more times, trying to shake the plug, then disappeared.

Five minutes later Wilkey hooked the last tarpon of the day, one that went about twenty-five pounds. The tired fish was coming grudgingly to the boat when the hooks pulled out.

Companions Discreetly Silent When Hunter Has Bad Day

Statesboro, Georgia

The big dog stopped in midstride and snapped into a beautiful point on the edge of the field.

"Your bird, Mr. Bryant," said Wendell Marsh, who, with his brother Hugh, runs the Marsh Hunting Preserve, eight miles northwest of Statesboro.

I moved in, the quail flushed and flew straight away, an easy shot, and for the fourth consecutive time I missed. My fellow hunter, Waymon Reese, the administrator of the Bulloch County Hospital in Statesboro, waited a moment, then dropped the bird.

It was one of those calamitous days that befall every bird hunter, a day when something goes wrong with timing and misses continue, the tension mounts, and companions, who at first chide you good-naturedly, studiously avoid looking you in the eye.

The time-honored procedure is to laugh at yourself and offer excuses. If you are using a borrowed gun, as I wasn't, your excuse is already made. Otherwise, you can refer to a light touch of bursitis, or if that is too humdrum, hint that the piece of shrapnel you took in your shoulder in Normandy is taking its toll.

You can also stare at the shotgun in your hands as if it were some strange piece of equipment you had never seen before. This, of course, is the same gun you proudly displayed to your companions at the start of the hunt, perhaps intimating that you and it were a deadly combination.

Running true to form, I glared at the lovely little L. C. Smith 20-gauge double I carried, then whipped it to my shoulder a few times, sighting at an imaginary quail.

Marsh and Reese watched me covertly; then Marsh indicated he would like to handle the gun.

He looked it over, brought it up to shooting position, then lowered it slowly and returned it to me saying, "Mr. Bryant, that sure is a poor way to treat such a pretty little gun."

It should be made clear that Marsh and I had quickly established an easy rapport. If we had not done so he would have been the perfect Southern gentleman, offering suggestions on whether I was shooting high or low or behind only if he thought I was in the mood for it.

His humor, whether or not it was intended as therapy, proved efficacious, and for the remainder of the day the little gun and I got along rather well, although we had no chance of catching up with Reese.

Reese had hunted the area with his father a few days. "The old gentleman had a fine time with us, didn't he, Mr. Reese?" asked Marsh as we followed the pointers through some pines.

"He certainly did. He's sixty-eight, you know. He did some pretty good shooting. Shot twenty-four out of twenty-five."

I held my lovely little gun close and said nothing.

Excess Goulash
Entices King Mackerel
to the Hook

Marathon, Florida

King mackerel like goulash. Whether they would enjoy it as a steady diet is another matter, one that would require additional research.

It all began when Kamil "Sport" DeGrechie of Schuylerville, New York, prepared a goulash for three fellow fishermen. It was a good goulash, a sterling goulash. We ate it for supper, breakfast, and lunch, and even then half a gallon of it remained.

We could have consumed it in one more breakfast, and our failure to do so did not mean that we did not find it good, but goulash is like love: too much is cloying.

It was DeGrechie himself who put the remaining goulash in a plastic bag and announced that he was going to use it to chum king mackerel. Chumming is a time-honored technique for attracting fish. To chum fish is to toss small scraps of food, usually ground or cut fish, into the water. If everything works right, the fish you are seeking are attracted by the chum, move in, and seize your bait.

Chumming can be done from shore or from a boat. More than half a century ago anglers at the exclusive fishing club at Pasque Island (one of the Elizabeth Islands off Massachusetts) used to chum striped bass from shore with chunks of menhaden, then catch them with strips of the same fish. As a boy fishing out of my father's boat off Martha's Vineyard Island more than thirty years ago, my spindly arms ached from turning the handle of a huge meat grinder that was mounted on the stern and fed with chunks of trash fish.

Chumming is very much in evidence off Florida. One may now purchase frozen blocks of ground-up fish. These blocks are placed in a net bag hung in the water.

DeGrechie did not ask our skipper, John Caperonis of Saratoga Springs, New York, to eschew the use of the commercial chum. He merely suggested that we supplement the conventional material with his home cooking.

That day the boat took more kings than it had any day in the previous week, and on the following trip, without goulash, we caught no kings at all.

He said he could not remember the precise recipe for his goulash. However, we did note that it contained olive oil, onions, green peppers, whole canned tomatoes, noodles, and hamburger.

DeGrechie is a man of many talents. In addition to being a good cook, he knows many home cures. Caperonis, for example, had driven a fish spine into his big toe and no amount of probing could locate it. The toe grew large, sore, and red.

"Wrap it in salt pork," said DeGrechie, "and the pork will draw it out."

Caperonis wore a slab of salt pork on his toe for two days. At the end of that time the redness localized and the offending half-inch-long spine rose up out of the angry flesh and was easily withdrawn with tweezers.

This treatment would be awkward if one had to wear shoes over the pork.

Off Posh Cat Cay's Lee Shore
Fisherman Lands a Barracuda

Cat Cay, Bahamas

His lean flanks gleaming in the bright afternoon sun, a three-foot barracuda twisted out of the water twice before we brought him to gaff and gingerly plucked the silver spoon he had mistaken for a bait fish from his long, sharp-toothed jaws.

"There will be more," said our skipper, John Samson of Fort Lauderdale, Florida, as he ran his whaler close to the eastern shore of Gun Cay. Before the afternoon was over and we returned to the harbor at Cat Cay, Arnold Rotsman of New York City and I had caught two more barracuda, two houndfish, and a blue runner.

Our catch was no cause for jubilation, but under the circumstances it was the best we could do. A stiff southwest breeze and heavy seas kept us from venturing forth on the windward side of the island and also made it impractical to try for bonefish on the vast flats that extend from Cat Cay harbor to South Cat Cay.

Having taken some severe jouncing while hugging the lee shore of the islands, we were interested in learning how the other members of our party had fared, for they had gone out into the open water northwest of Cat Cay in two larger boats, for marlin and other oceanic fish.

They had, we discovered, stayed with it for about four hours until more than half of them were seasick, boating several barracuda and a thirty-pound wahoo.

John "Boog" Powell, the Baltimore Orioles' massive first baseman, caught the wahoo, and this was as it should have been, for Powell was participating as a guest in the filming of a segment of an hour-long Columbia Broadcasting System television special, "Fisherman's World," which will be shown from 5 to 6 P.M., New York time, February 21. Those aboard the two boats included Powell's pretty, dark-haired wife, Janet, and the former Hollywood actor John Bromfield, who will be host for the show, which is being produced for C.B.S. by Fenton McHugh Productions, Inc., of Chicago, with Vic Dunaway, former outdoor editor of the Miami *Herald,* as technical advisor.

In the evening, in the Cat Cay Club dining room following their rough experience, the battered fishermen had recovered sufficiently to enjoy broiled steaks cut from Powell's wahoo, and as a form of insurance for the following day, Dunaway dispensed anti-motion-sickness pills to all hands.

Cat Cay, a lush island on the western edge of the Grand Bahamas Bank, is a little more than two miles long and a half mile wide, and thirty-five minutes by air from Miami via Chalk's Flying Service, which operates daily flights to Cat Cay and Bimini with amphibious planes.

Since 1914 Cat Cay has been in the hands of one or more wealthy Americans and is presently owned by a group brought together by Willard F. Rockwell, Jr., board chairman of North American Rockwell.

Through most of the thirties, forties, and fifties, what was perhaps the most exclusive and expensive club in the English-speaking world flourished on Cat Cay, frequented by actors and actresses, millionaires, captains of industry, and titled Englishmen.

By 1964 the club had ceased to exist, and most of its property —buildings, docks, golf and tennis courts, skeet and trap ranges— had fallen into deep disrepair, which was hastened by Hurricane Betsy in 1965.

Rockwell and his fellow investors bought the island last May, and since then much of what had been allowed to deteriorate has been rebuilt and there have been many improvements, including the new reinforced concrete docks in the harbor.

Men of wealth including Marshall Field, Jr., Roger S. Firestone, and August A. Busch are new equity members of Cat Cay Club, Ltd., whose address, for those who might be interested, is P. O. Box 723, Buena Vista Station, Miami, Florida 33137.

Rainy North Carolina Day Opportunity to Meet Adolph

Charlotte, North Carolina

All day cold rain driven by a sharp northeast wind swept across Mack Ballard's one-hundred-acre Squash Hill Shooting Preserve.

Quail hunting was out of the question, but the day was far from lost. It was a good opportunity, among other things, to meet Adolph, one of Charlotte's better-known citizens. Adolph is aging and rather grizzled, but senility is still far away for this nine-year-old Drahthaar, Ballard's remarkable hunting dog.

Adolph's breed—which includes pointer, French poodle, otter hound, and foxhound—is about a century old according to Ballard, who estimates that there are fewer than five thousand of the animals in the United States. The breed is usually versatile. Adolph will point and retrieve quail, pheasant, and woodcock, and will retrieve ducks and hunt deer.

Before opening the preserve four years ago with his partner, Elliott Newcombe, Ballard ran a sporting goods store in Charlotte. There Adolph soon demonstrated that he could wait on customers in a limited way. He could, for example, distinguish between packages of round and square crackers and apparently is able to count.

"Many of my customers knew Adolph's name, but not mine,"

Ballard said. "They came to see him. I never trained him to do those things or to point or retrieve. I don't try to understand it."

One might have been inclined to attribute these stories of Adolph's prowess to Ballard's obvious love for the animal. But all through that wet, cold day, Ballard's friends dropped in at the hunting camp near the entrance to the preserve to talk of dogs and birds, and all confirmed his stories.

At one point, while Adolph lay sleeping in the sawdust near the stove, Ballard took a cardboard box and walked a quarter of a mile down the road in the rain and hid the box in the grass. After his return, he awakened Adolph and said, with no gesturing and in a conversational tone: "Adolph, I left a box down the road a piece. Would you get it for me?"

Adolph smiled, nodded, and fetched the box.

"You've got to stay another day and see him work birds," Ballard said, a sentiment that was echoed by Newcombe and J. Haynes Lassiter of Charlotte, when they dropped in for lunch.

In Charlotte that evening Lassiter and his charming wife whetted our appetites for the following day's hunt with a forty-five-minute documentary film on quail.

Squash Hill, about a half-hour's drive from the Charlotte Airport, is an excellent preserve, offering both quail and pheasants. Hunters may bring their own dogs or hunt over Ballard's Drahthaars or pointers. The address is Box 9381, Charlotte.

Mineral Box a Shining Goal, But Reaching It Means Nothing

Marco Island, Florida

We paddled down a canal in the Everglades under a wide blue sky and against a brisk breeze, plugging for largemouth bass.

For the first mile and a half we did not work too hard at angling because a tipster in the Collier County sheriff's office had told us that the fishing wouldn't be good until we reached a mineral box on the west bank.

The mineral box became a goal, a promise of many things glorious, and many objects sighted in the distance and identified as the mineral box proved to be something else.

Finally, its roof gleaming against a dark background of trees, the mineral box (a shedlike structure that contains salt and other minerals for cattle to eat) appeared and we paddled harder.

We drew abreast of it and went past, and no fish struck. We fished with great dedication for a few hours, leaving the mineral box far behind, throwing plugs and weedless spoons and worms against the grass and reeds along the shore. By noon one of our party, John Wilhelm of the Florida Development Commission, had caught one small largemouth. Neither Fred Archibald, Wilhelm's right-hand man, nor I had raised a fish.

Lunch provided a welcome break, and we pulled the canoe onto the shore beside the rippling waters of the canal and ate, using a paddle blade for a table.

Refreshed, we set forth on the return trip and went past the mineral box without comment. Before reaching our jeep, which was parked at the junction of Florida's Alligator Alley and the canal, we caught one more small bass.

Although the trip had consumed most of the day, Wilhelm and Archibald did not despair, and on our way to Marco Island we spotted tarpon rolling in a small pond off Route 92, Marco's link to the mainland.

As the sun was setting we hooked several tarpon and a few snook. The tarpon were everywhere, rolling on the surface, but were not, according to Wilhelm, feeding with genuine enthusiasm.

"If they were really hungry, we would have gotten a hit on every cast," he said.

None of us tied into a really large fish. The average was about eight pounds. But there were some good-sized fellows, up to perhaps sixty pounds, sporting in that little roadside pond.

"Oh, how I wish I had time to investigate all these ponds and sloughs and canals," said Wilhelm. "There are fish everywhere, fish that the average fellow can reach without an expensive boat or a guide."

Marco Island Guide Knows Jig Should Be Sweetened With Shrimp

Marco Island, Florida

Doyle Doxsee maneuvered his twenty-foot inboard launch at high speed through the narrow channels between the mangrove islands until he reached a little cove that resembled a hundred others we had passed.

Tossing the anchor overboard, he motioned toward the shore and said, "Try it right there."

We were using light spinning rods and bucktail jigs sweetened with small pieces of shrimp.

He was fast to a jack crevalle on his second cast, and I followed with a snook. Both fish, indeed all fish caught that day, were returned to the water.

The jack, which resembles a portly bluefish, is poor eating, and few fishermen keep them. The snook is a fine food fish, but neither Doxsee nor I was fishing for food.

Doxsee, who is a native of the island and a fishing guide, wastes no time in one spot when the fishing is slow. If ten or twenty casts produce little action, the anchor comes up and he is on his way.

Being unable to observe any particular pattern in the areas he fished except that, as one might expect, all casts were made right at the base of the mangroves, I asked why he chose one place over another.

"I just know. Years ago we fished commercially for mullet around these islands. Used gill nets. We learned where the fish are," he replied.

His knowledge proved sound. All through the day we caught and released a variety of finny prey, ranging from the snook and jack crevalle to slim, silvery, hard-fighting ladyfish, redfish, mangrove snappers, gafftopsail catfish, and sea trout (weakfish). We also spotted a few tarpon rolling but did not try for them.

All were caught on shrimp-baited bucktails, which we bounced along the bottom. "You can try a plug if you want, but you probably won't do anything with it at this time of year," Doxsee said, and he was right.

As we moved through the mangrove islands we surprised a variety of birds, including ducks, cormorants, pelicans, egrets, and an American bald eagle.

On Marco Island itself there are, according to Bryan Donaldson of the public relations department of the Marco Island Development Corporation, three active American eagle nests, including one in a pine tree on the golf course.

Marco is on the Gulf Coast of Florida, about twenty-seven miles south of Naples, at the northern end of the ten-thousand-islands area, which runs south into the Everglades. The waters around Marco are for everything a light-tackle angler could ask.

The island, roughly ten miles long and five miles wide, is currently involved in a spectacular land and building boom. Prime cause for this is the Marco Island Development Corporation, which owns most of the island. It is another of the planned communities being developed by Florida's Mackle Brothers, Frank, Jr., Elliott, and Robert.

Pithy Tales and Latin Phrases Flow from Everglades Guide

Moore Haven, Florida

George L. Espenlaub, the lean, weathered seventy-year-old guide whose bullfrog larynx handles Latin and pithy tales of his beloved Everglades with equal facility, picked the sable palm he wanted and assailed it with a hatchet.

His goal was the heart of the palm, as it is known in some restaurants, or swamp cabbage, as it is called by Florida woodsmen. In five minutes he had a two-foot-long white cylinder, four or five inches in diameter, in his hand, a substantial portion of which was the main course of our campfire lunch at Fish-eating Creek. The palm heart was cut in small pieces and boiled in water along with chunks of smoked bacon, potatoes, and onions, making a rich and tasty stew. For an appetizer we had goobers—green peanuts boiled in brine.

Espenlaub, whose address is Box 301, Clewiston, Florida, takes Audubon groups and others on tours of the 300,000-acre Fish-eating Creek Wildlife Refuge, which is owned by the Lykes brothers. Beef cattle (Florida is second only to Texas in the production of beef cattle) are raised on the refuge.

"Ask me the common name or the Latin name of any flora or fauna you see, and I'll tell you forthwith," rumbled Espenlaub as we drove through wide meadows, cypress swamps, and palm groves in our jeep, and he did.

The party also included John Wilhelm and Fred Archibald of the Florida Development Commission, and Ned Moren of Clearwater, Florida. Moren once was known as the Pied Piper of Pinellas County. He came by this title because of his ability to catch rattlesnakes alive. Working on a contract from the county, he caught five thousand rattlers in one year. His record for one day, which still stands in Florida, was sixty-eight snakes. (Live rattlers are sold to zoos or exhibitors, and their venom, used to prepare snakebite serum, is milked from them. The meat of rattlers is often canned.)

Wilhelm and Archibald opened the day with a visit to a man Wilhelm described as the "poet laureate of Fish-eating Creek," the Reverend Robey Ward, a retired Baptist minister. The Reverend Mr. Ward and his wife camp on the refuge every winter. Standing in the bright dawn with the sun gleaming on his white hair, the charming old gentleman recited a pastoral poem as the pungent smoke from the dried palmetto leaves in the outdoor fire where the Wards do all their cooking drifted about us.

We also caught largemouth bass and pickerel in the creek, climbed trees for wild oranges and lemons, inspected the Fort Center Indian Mound, which is being excavated by the department of anthropology of Florida Atlantic University, saw the smallest wild orchid on the North American continent, saw rare burrowing owls, buzzards, American bald eagles, ospreys, wild turkeys, white ibises, Audubon's caracara (a hawklike bird), Wilson's snipe, widgeon, blue-winged teal, mallards, American egrets, and cattle egrets.

Jamaica's Mountain Mullet Man Proves Singularly Elusive

Ocho Rios, Jamaica

Two small yellow birds flew onto the terrace of my room at the Plantation Inn, which overlooks the Caribbean, and seemed to expect a share of my breakfast.

They took bits of toast from my hand as a warm, onshore wind stirred in the coconut palms below and pushed small waves on the white beach.

The yellow birds had transferred their attention to the marmalade when a brace of big black birds, whose eyes looked like rifle targets, arrived and drove the others away.

Lying about ninety miles south of Cuba, an hour and twenty minutes by jet from Miami, Jamaica is lush and many-rivered, 150 miles long, and equal in area to Connecticut. A series of mountain ridges, the highest peak 7,520 feet above sea level, runs east and west along the island's middle.

Jamaica has almost all the shallow-water and offshore species of fish one finds in Florida or the Bahamas, and an article last summer in *The Daily Gleaner* of Kingston, Jamaica, told of a little-known freshwater fish called the mountain mullet. According to *The Gleaner,* one A. J. Thomas, a former fisheries expert for the

Jamaican Government, was the island's mullet expert, and had taken them on a fly rod.

To catch a wily mountain mullet seemed a worthwhile project, but Thomas proved, during a series of phone calls from Ocho Rios to Kingston, to be as elusive as the fish.

A call to *The Gleaner* produced the suggestion that I call the Ministry of Agriculture and Fisheries. A spokesman for that agency said that Thomas had moved since returning from his duties abroad with the Food and Agriculture Organization of the United Nations, and suggested that I call the home of a Mr. Smith, who was related to Thomas. At the Smith home the soft female Jamaican voice that answered could barely be heard over the poor connection, but it seemed as if she said that she knew where Mr. Thomas lived but did not know his telephone number. At that point the connection failed completely.

There were four listings for Thomases whose first name began with A in Kingston, the operator said. I called them all. There was no answer at the first three. The fourth number produced someone who said he was the home of Mr. A. J. Thomas. But he added a note of doubt: "I have been working here only two weeks."

"My Mr. Thomas was at one time with the fisheries division," I said.

"Oh, no, sir, Mr. Thomas is a cabinetmaker," the voice replied.

I thanked him and said good-by.

My breakfast companions, the two yellow birds, flew into the room and perched on a brightly colored basket of flowers hanging from the wall. A large mothlike insect with jet black wings, touched with fiery orange where they joined his body, drifted in from the terrace on the gentle sea wind, then flew out over the green Caribbean, dark against the bright blue sky.

Avocado Pear Not Ripe Enough for Fastidious Mountain Mullet

Ocho Rios, Jamaica

Leaning my fly rod against a coconut palm—the last time it had been out of its case was in Labrador—I watched Austen J. Thomas striving to catch a mountain mullet before daylight failed.

Thomas, a former fisheries expert for the Jamaican government who has recently returned from an assignment in West Africa with the Food and Agriculture Organization of the United Nations, is Jamaica's expert on the mountain mullet, a freshwater fish whose scientific name is *Agonostomus Monticola.*

At the Plantation Inn, with Deryck Roberts of the Jamaica Tourist Board, the man who had brought us together, Thomas gave me a cram course on Jamaica's sport and commercial fisheries and then asked gently, "You, sir, are particularly interested in mountain mullet?"

"Could we catch one?" I asked.

"This is not the best time of the year. They spawn at sea in winter and return to the rivers later. They are a splendid food fish and a good sporting fish. I have caught two over four pounds."

"I have an extra fly rod in my room," I said, and he was hooked.

281

"We could try. There is a river nearby. But we will need a ripe avocado pear."

"Why will we need a pear?"

"Ripe avocado is the best bait. Shrimp is all right, but pear is the best. One could fish a long time for mullet uselessly if one had no pear. I never send someone to the market to buy my pear and I often visit several places before I find the right one."

We hied to a fruit and vegetable market in Ocho Rios.

"Have you a ripe pear?" Thomas asked a woman at one of the booths.

"I have a pear which will be ripe tomorrow morning," she said, handing it to him.

Thomas pressed the pear with a thumb and shook his head dubiously, saying to me, "We may have to find another pear. Let me borrow your penknife."

He made two deep incisions in the pear, while several of the women gathered about, and lifted a segment from it. "Madam, I do not doubt your word," he said, "but this pear must be right."

He smelled the cut-out piece, then bit into it. "It may do," he said.

Half an hour later, at a nearby river, we found a small boy, eleven-year-old Derick Jones, who volunteered to guide for us and to catch us some shrimp for bait if the pear failed, and we were fishing shortly before sunset.

Thomas used a No. 10 hook baited with a small piece of pear and soon had a hit, but failed to hook the fish. "The pear is not ripe enough. It is too hard for the fish to get at the hook," he said.

We were working the last likely-looking pool when a band of Jamaican boys came through the palms for an evening swim.

"I am sorry," said Thomas, reeling in. "If we had time I could show you several very good mountain mullet streams. Please come back."

We shook hands in the gathering twilight, and he and Roberts began their long trip to Kingston. I got into my car, and forgetting for a moment to stay to the left, nearly hit a truckload of men heading home from work. They seemed more amused than frightened, I noted, as I hauled hard to port and crept toward the Plantation Inn.